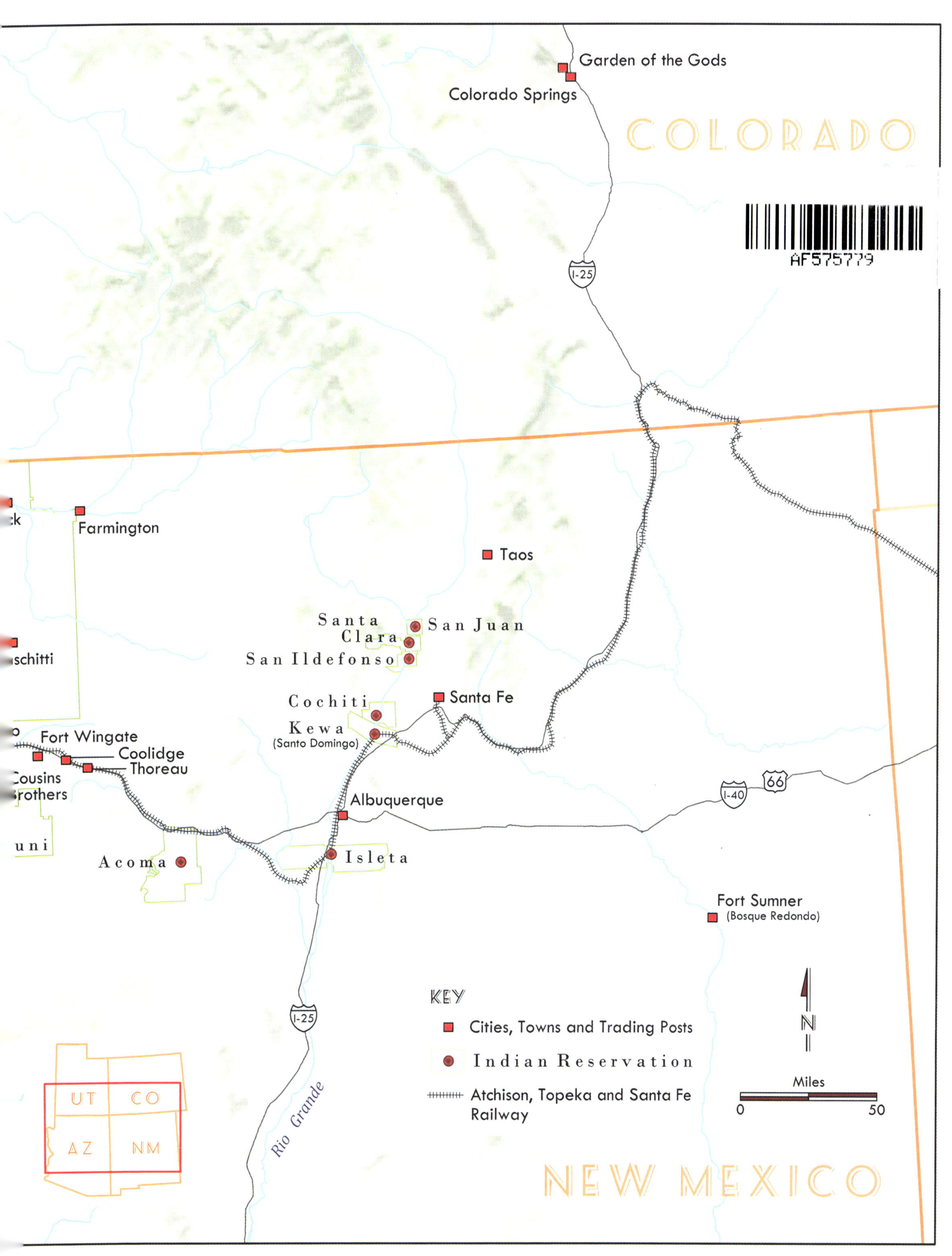
Garden of the Gods
Colorado Springs
COLORADO
I-25
Farmington
Taos
Santa Clara
San Juan
San Ildefonso
Cochiti
Santa Fe
Kewa
(Santo Domingo)
Fort Wingate
Coolidge
Thoreau
Albuquerque
I-40
66
Acoma
Isleta
Fort Sumner
(Bosque Redondo)
I-25
KEY
Cities, Towns and Trading Posts
Indian Reservation
Atchison, Topeka and Santa Fe Railway
N
Miles
0
50
UT
CO
AZ
NM
Rio Grande
NEW MEXICO

Reassessing
HALLMA
of
NATIVE
JE
Artists, Traders,
Pat Me
Est.
SCHIFFER
PUBLISHING
1974
Inspiring through expert knowledge

Library of Congress Control Number: 2014939560

Cover & Book Designed by Danielle D. Farmer
Type set in Canter/Baffled/Frutiger LT Std

ISBN: 978-0-7643-4670-5
Printed in India
10 9 8 7 6 5 4 3 2

Published by Schiffer Publishing, Ltd.
4880 Lower Valley Road
Atglen, PA 19310
Phone: (610) 593-1777; Fax: (610) 593-2002
E-mail: Info@schifferbooks.com

Barton Wright, 1920–2011

During the preparation for this volume, we lost one of our greatest supporters when Barton Wright passed away in March 2011. Barton was not only a good friend but a patient mentor. We were honored that such a respected authority on Hopi culture and arts would openly share his knowledge with non-academics such as ourselves. Over the years, from the mid-1990s until his passing, we never ceased to enjoy time spent with Barton and his wife, Margaret, not only discussing the first peoples of the Americas, but also sharing laughs and good Mexican food. Besides the research he freely shared with us, perhaps one of his most important pieces of advice was to write down any bit of valuable information we ran across and to put it in a shoebox. When we look now at our file boxes stuffed with research notes, we think of Barton's advice and wonder if it was a blessing or a curse.

We miss his spirit, humor, and unrelenting faith in our efforts.

Pat and Kim Messier
Tucson, Arizona

CONTENTS

FOREWORD

Much has been written about Southwest Indian jewelry, beginning with Washington Matthews in the 1880s, but individual silversmiths received little serious attention until John Adair's 1944 book *Navajo and Pueblo Silversmiths*. It was not until the 1970s that the identity of the individual silversmith gained wide importance to the buying public. Since then, there have been a number of books on hallmarks and on jewelers that vary in reliability. Over time some writers have simply repeated what earlier writers said about artists, and in doing so, they unwittingly, even carelessly, repeated incorrect information. Factual information about some artists that was generally known in the 1940s and 1950s, even the 1960s, began to dissipate in a wave of digital repetition of errors. But truth does not lie in consensus, and an authoritative voice cannot substitute for sound research.

Beginning in the mid-1950s, I traveled with my father to Indian arts shows where he served as a judge, to trading posts, to the homes of artists, and to the stores of long-established Indian art dealers (most now gone), and now I have been in the Indian arts business for a little shy of 50 years (my first solo buying trip was at age 16). Consequently, the growth of what I call "myth-information" in this, the Information Age has been a particular source of irritation to me (and to many of the artists and their families).

In interviewing Roger Skeet Jr. some years ago, the first thing he did was produce a copy of the C. G. Wallace Auction catalog and turn to dog-eared pages to show where his and his father's work had been misattributed. It was clearly a sore point and he wanted the record corrected.

Happily, this volume addresses and corrects a number of instances of misattribution of hallmarks as well as certain details about the lives of many of the artists. Their research is thorough and the conclusions are irrefutable. Clear photos of both jewelry and hallmarks are further enhanced by useful and interesting contextual information about the artists (and businesses, in the case of shop hallmarks). In the process, the authors have provided the reader with a better, more accurate sense of the relationships between the artists and the dealers, the dealers and the market.

If that sounds like a dry assessment, I apologize: this is a fascinating read for those interested in Indian jewelry of the twentieth century and the men and women who produced it.

Mark Bahti
Southwestern scholar,
writer, and shop owner

• • •

Jewelry found on an ancient sunken ship makes headlines everywhere. The opening of a new exhibit of the gold of Troy brings hundreds of people to view it. Adornments of many kinds have been used for centuries, from a stone with a hole drilled in it that is strung on a cord to make a pendant, to an elaborate diadem of gold. The value to the owner ranges from the simple pleasure of a wearer to the heightened esteem of a ruler. Jewelry might serve like the plumage of the Bird of Paradise does to make one attractive to a prospective mate, or become a sacred religious or ritual piece. Before the advent of metal, individuals were adept at using the materials available in their environment, from clay beads to colorful minerals and seashells.

The discovery of iron and the ability to work it brought about the use of silver and gold to fashion prized jewelry in many parts of the world. European settlers in what is now the United States brought with them their metalworking knowledge. The use of silver among the indigenous Indians spread by contact with metalsmiths and by dealing with the fur and hide traders across the country. In the Southwest, native metalsmiths emerged in the 1800s. As the use of silver grew popular among southwestern tribes, varying styles emerged, from the hammered and cast pieces set with turquoise among the Navajos to the fine stone inlay of the Zuni and the silver overlay of the Hopi craftsman.

I was about twelve when my family, on one of our regular sightseeing trips, drove from Conejos County in Colorado down along the Rio Grande River to Santa Fe. There, as well as enjoying the paintings of the Santa Fe artists and the beautiful black and polychrome pottery of the Pueblo Indians, we admired the silver and turquoise jewelry made by Indian craftsmen. My father bought me a lovely little silver and turquoise bracelet. This began my lifelong enjoyment of beautiful handmade Indian silver jewelry. Later, I was able to spend much time in the Hopi villages and become acquainted with a number of the silversmiths, including several of the early ones and their friends and relatives. I was fortunate to hear many stories about them, which put faces behind the bracelets. Jimmy Kewanwytewa told of his brother, Pierce, and cousin, Ralph Tawangyouma, who as teenage boys used a blowtorch to melt the solder off of tin cans and then try to make jewelry from it (many, many cans!). They both became skilled silversmiths.

Pat and Kim Messier have compiled a book including these two silversmiths and many others among the Indians of the Southwest. They have traced the workers from before the use of hallmarks to the present, and also have beautiful photographs of many pieces of jewelry. They discuss in great depth the economic growth of this craft, from the making of a single piece of jewelry for oneself to a worldwide market on the Internet. This fine book is an excellent guide to the enjoyment of southwestern Indian jewelry.

Margaret Wright
Author of *Hopi Silver:*
The History and Hallmarks of
Hopi Silversmithing

PREFACE

After decades of research into American Indian art, our first publication, *Hopi & Pueblo Tiles,* became reality in 2007. The following year, we enthusiastically began another project, not realizing how much more difficult a jewelry book would be; nor did we comprehend how frustrating—and rewarding—would be our decision to do all the photography ourselves for this project. It quickly became a much more ambitious endeavor than the tile book, and the thought of attempting to add a meaningful and useful title to the established literature of American Indian jewelry became daunting. We were certain, however, that our research was significant and that it would be valuable to the Indian art community and jewelry collectors.

Our initial research focused on early hallmarked Hopi silverwork; the makers of these pieces were men who left their homes on the Hopi mesas to work in curio shops across the country. Yet our research did not stop with Hopi silver, as we soon became fascinated by many early silversmiths who signed their work. We also found it crucial to understand the roles played by various organizations in the development of Indian jewelry. The Indian Arts and Crafts Board (IACB) and the United Indian Traders Association (UITA) are two whose efforts to "salvage" handmade Indian jewelry from machine-made competition has been obscured over the years because documentation is lacking. The late Barton Wright and the late Tom Woodard attempted to piece together the records of the UITA silver stamping program, but found it so poorly documented they had little success. Somewhat better documented, though still far from complete, are the various guilds and cooperatives—such as the Navajo Guild and the Hopi Silvercraft Guild—which helped guide some tribal communities to achieve control over the fate of their own arts.

During the early decades of the twentieth century, Indian jewelry was deemed a curio item; consequently, little information pertaining to hallmarks was recorded or documented at that time. Therefore, a great deal is owed to the research done in the 1970s and 1980s by Barton Wright and Margaret Wright. Contemporary collectors would know far less than they do if it were not for their tireless efforts to record the hallmarks of Indian silversmiths. Today, it would be impossible to reconstruct the information they gathered, and many facts would surely be lost as most of the traders and silversmiths concerned have passed away.

This book is not intended to be all-inclusive—or to replace the venerable references *Hallmarks of the Southwest* and *Hopi Silver.* It is meant to supplement the knowledge of American Indian jewelry. After discussions with collectors, traders, and academics, we realized we could contribute to the current understanding of the hallmarks applied to Indian jewelry. There are still many unknown hallmarks that need to be identified, and we hope this publication opens the door to more extensive research.

ACKNOWLEDGMENTS

Thanks are due to many individuals who have graciously helped with this project over the years—without you, this book would not have been possible. We extend our apologies to anyone we may have overlooked who has contributed to our research.

We are thankful to Karen Sires for her generosity in sharing items from her extensive collection.

Thanks to Mark Bahti for his friendship and tireless efforts in sourcing information and for obtaining signed documents.

We greatly appreciate the generosity of the following persons who shared their collections: Julia White, Doris Roland, Russell Hartman, Madeleine Nash, Robert and Judy Farling, Pam Evans, Michael Schultz, David and Melinda West of Gallery West, and Jamie Way and Jed Foutz of Shiprock Santa Fe.

We thank the artists who were generous with their time: Liz Wallace, Cippy CrazyHorse, Lawrence and Griselda Saufkie, Anthony Lovato, Joel Pajarito, Cordell Pajarito, Mary C. Lovato, Sedelio F. Lovato, Julian Lovato, Edison Cummings, Howard and Patricia Sice, Perry Shorty, Kee Yazzie Jr., Roy Talahaftewa, Frank Patania Jr., Sam Patania, and Jason Garcia.

We are grateful to the staff at Arizona State Museum, especially Diane Dittemore, Alan Ferg, Jannelle Weakly, Mike Jacobs, Teresa Moreno, and Mary E. Graham. At the Heard Museum, Diana Pardue and Mario Nick Klimiades; Jonathan Batkin and Cheri Falkenstien-Doyle at the Wheelwright Museum; Diane Bird of the Museum of New Mexico/Laboratory of Anthropology; Russell Hartman, Kelly Jensen, and Rebecca Morin at California Academy of Sciences; and Deborah Slaney of the Albuquerque Museum.

The following have provided their support, advice, guidance, or expertise over the years: Margaret and Barton Wright, Tom Woodard, Robert Bauver, Robert Gallegos, John Hill, Gene Waddell, Darlene and Robert Seng, Jeff Ogg, Karen Barrie, Allan and Carol Hayes, Susan O'Bryen Phillips, Jane Q. Peterson, Tobi Lopez Taylor, Catherine Gilman, Paula Baxter and Barry Katzen, Amy Hammarstrom, Emmi Whitehorse, Sue Voss, Joan Mathys, Rosalee Anderson, Nancy Wilson, John and Gloria Garcia, Judy Boebert, Paddy Schwartz, Lynda Shoemaker, Dennis June, Carolyn O'Bagy Davis, Garden of the Gods Trading Post, Ernie Bulow, Joe and Janice Day, and Milland Lomakema Sr.

Special thanks to Pat Cattani for her help with the manuscript.

Many thanks to Nancy Schiffer, of Schiffer Publishing, for her support in making this book a reality, as well as to the helpful staff.

Note: Unless otherwise indicated the objects illustrated in this book are from the authors' collection.

iNTRODUCTiON

Sometimes more can be discerned from the back of a piece of antique American Indian jewelry than from the front. Not only can construction methods be determined, but occasionally the origin can also be revealed. The back or underside may contain stamped or scratched marks, generally letters or symbols, which denote by whom or where the piece was made. These marks are commonly termed "hallmarks."

Stamped hallmark of bow and arrow used by Ike Wilson (Navajo). *Courtesy White collection.*

Scratched-in raincloud and "H" hallmark used by Ralph Tawangyawma (Hopi).

Hallmarking by the designer or maker of handcrafted objects of precious metals has been a common practice the world over for centuries. Though the term "hallmark" is conventionally used to denote marks applied by official or governmental agencies, it has become synonymous with individual makers' marks where American Indian jewelry is concerned.

American Indians of the Southwest, however, did not initially follow this practice of applying identifying marks to their silver objects for a variety of reasons. Mainly, it was not the custom of these peoples to sign their handcrafted wares because their arts and crafts had previously been made for daily use within their own community or for barter with their neighbors. But in the late 1800s, their lifestyles changed with the introduction of a cash economy as non-indigenous people flooded the Arizona and New Mexico territories. Their crafts then became a means of obtaining money, sold to an outside market and no longer just for their own use.

At the turn of the twentieth century, an explosion of interest in American Indian arts and crafts took place. These early collectors were uninterested in the identity of the artist; they only cared that the object look authentically primitive. As tourism increased in the American Southwest, jewelry became one of the most popular curio items. The demand for Indian jewelry outstripped the supply, and several businesses sprang up to mechanically mass-produce lightweight, inexpensive silver jewelry in a style that most tourists believed was authentic.

Shop mark used by Garden of the Gods Trading Post.

Some curio shops with Indian silversmiths in their employ created marks that were applied to the jewelry made in their workshops; these are referred to as "shop marks." They served to show their jewelry had been handmade in an effort to combat the machine-made Indian-style jewelry dominating the market.

Stamped hallmark used by Fred Peshlakai (Navajo). *Courtesy Karen Sires.*

Stamped hallmark of coyote head and "H" used by Grant Jenkins (Hopi).

Chiseled hallmark of JD used by Juan De Dios (Zuni). *Courtesy Karen Sires.*

A few individual silversmiths began signing their work in the late 1920s and early 1930s. Navajo Fred Peshlakai has often been credited with being the first silversmith to hallmark his work by the early 1930s. However, it has been documented that Juan De Dios of Zuni Pueblo used a chisel to stamp his initials on the back of some pieces in the late 1920s. Also Grant Jenkins, a Hopi silversmith, signed some of his pieces during his career from 1924 until his death in 1933. Perhaps prompted by their Anglo employers, many silversmiths who worked in urban areas also began signing their work in the 1930s, using symbols or their initials as identifying marks. Most of these early hallmarks were not documented because jewelry was usually considered to be nothing more than curio items.

After decades of growth and change in American Indian jewelry, it is now standard practice for Indian jewelers to sign their work with some kind of identification mark. Not only is there an active market for contemporary jewelers, but also for the work of recognized early silversmiths, which is in high demand. Even though books have been published that show and describe the marks used by many Indian silversmiths, the mistaken belief that hallmarks were not commonly applied to silver jewelry until the 1970s still persists. The general lack of hallmark documentation as recently as four decades ago resulted in much misinformation, and even respected authorities were misled about the identification of certain hallmarks. Combining extensive research with images of the hallmarks in context with the jewelry they were applied to, this book endeavors to correct some of the erroneous beliefs that continue to persist.

Birth and death dates of many of the artists in the text were obtained through the U.S. Indian Census Rolls, 1885–1940, and the Social Security Death Index, both available on Ancestry.com, as well as historic newspaper articles available at Newspaperarchive.com. The authors attempted to publish only information that could be substantiated by written documents. As much as possible, spellings of the Indian artists' names reflect their own preferences as used on business cards or other documents under their control.

Chapter 1:

OVERVIEW

The area known as the Colorado Plateau covers what is known today as the Four Corners region, where western Colorado, northern New Mexico, southeastern Utah, and northern Arizona meet. The southern portion of the plateau, with its mesas and canyons, was home to the ancestors of the modern Pueblo peoples of the Southwest. Centuries after the Ancestral Pueblo people settled into communal dwellings, an Athabaskan-speaking people migrated south into this area. The new residents were hunters and gatherers living in extended kinship groups; they called themselves Diné and are now known as the Navajo people.

Today the Pueblo people live in many culturally diverse villages, mostly near the Rio Grande River in northern New Mexico—Acoma, Laguna, and Zuni Pueblos are in western New Mexico. The Hopi people live on and around three mesas in northern Arizona. The Navajo now occupy the largest Indian reservation in the nation, encompassing most of northern Arizona and parts of New Mexico and Utah.

As humans have done since the dawn of time, the ancestors of the Pueblo and Navajo people created jewelry from natural materials. Stone, shell, bone, and even pottery fragments were fashioned into personal adornment, but by far the most treasured material was turquoise. Mined from various southwestern sites—especially in the Cerrillos area south of Santa Fe, New Mexico—turquoise was utilized in all forms of jewelry. It was a valuable item of trade and traveled a route from northern New Mexico through southern Arizona to Mesoamerica, with shells from the Pacific Ocean following the same route in reverse.

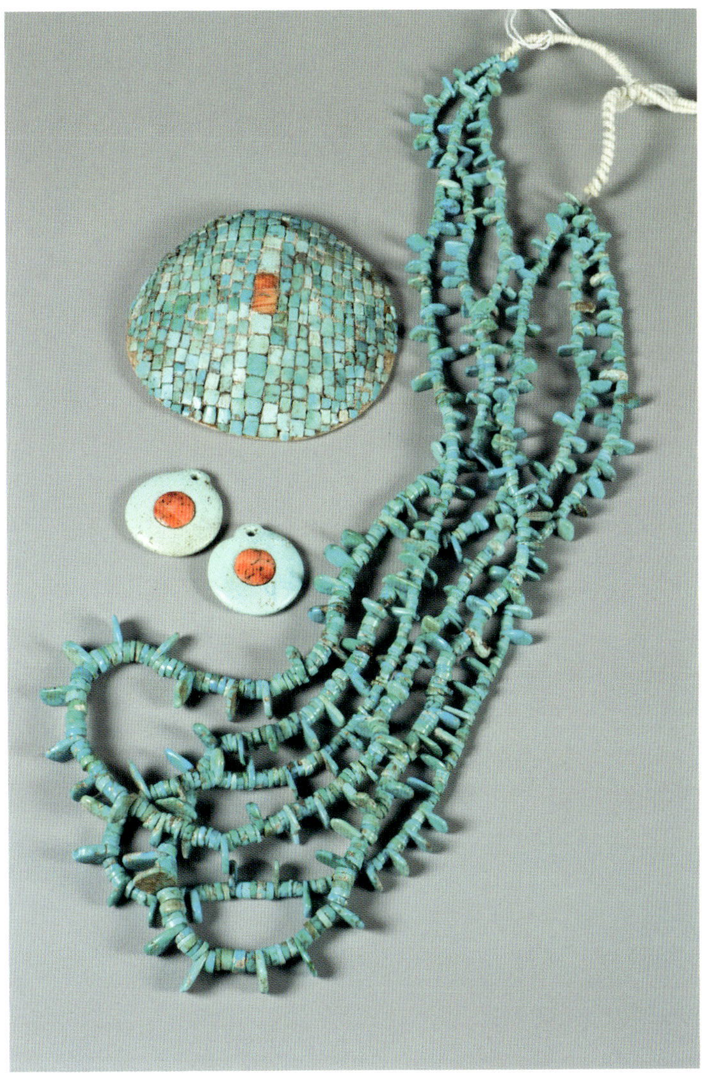

Examples of turquoise jewelry from three prehistoric Arizona cultures. Necklace, Hohokam, ASM# A-24171-C. Shell pendant with mosaic inlay of turquoise and spondylus, Mogollon, ASM# 6748. Earrings with spondylus inlays, Ancestral Puebloan, ASM# 431-A/431-B. *Courtesy Arizona State Museum, The University of Arizona.*

A selection of three pieces of jewelry from the collections of Arizona State Museum illustrates the use of turquoise in personal adornment by prehistoric Arizona cultures. A turquoise disk and tab necklace (c. 950–1150 AD), found loose in a pottery jar and recently restrung, is attributed to the Hohokam culture. Turquoise and spondylus shell were inlaid in a mosaic pattern upon a shell forming a pendant (c. 1225–1425 AD); the pendant was excavated at Kinishba Ruins, which was occupied by the Mogollon culture. The turquoise disk earrings with spondylus shell inlays (c. 450–1300 AD) were excavated in the Kayenta area occupied by Ancestral Pueblo people.

Jewelry worn by Hopi kachinas during ceremonial dances: silver *ketoh* (bow guard), leather bracelet with shells, and cottonwood earrings carved and painted to mimic turquoise mosaic earrings.

Jewelry was not only highly valued for personal adornment but also important for religious and ceremonial purposes. Necklaces, bracelets, earrings, and rings were worn for ceremonial dances and often buried with the deceased.

Early copper bracelets, Navajo or Ute. Twisted wire, ASM# 26566; flat wire, ASM# 22616; two round wire with file work, ASM# 12188 and 12189. *Courtesy Arizona State Museum, The University of Arizona.*

Photo of unknown silversmith at Laguna Pueblo, c. 1910.

When Europeans first traversed the American Southwest in the 1500s, they encountered people who had no metalworking capabilities, though they possessed copper bells traded from peoples farther south. Later, as Spanish colonists occupied the lands, the lifestyle of the native inhabitants was radically altered. Contact with Spanish and Mexican settlers provided access to metal tools and implements. By the 1830s, Navajo and Pueblo people were forming crude bracelets and ornaments from brass and copper wire. They learned the skill of working metal from Mexican blacksmiths in the mid-1800s, which would be adapted to working silver by the 1860s. Silver coins were hammered into form or melted into ingots that were then hammered to shape. The art of silversmithing spread quickly through the Rio Grande Pueblos and Zuni in the 1870s, but it was not introduced to the Hopis until 1898.

Squash blossom necklace owned by Hoskinini, considered the last chief of the Navajos, who gave it to Louisa Wetherill before his death in 1909. ASM# E-2311. *Courtesy Arizona State Museum, The University of Arizona.*

Concho by Hosteen Goodluck (Navajo). An important silversmith who worked from approximately late 1880s to early 1930s, he was a master of repoussé and fine stamp work. He did not mark his jewelry, but it can be attributed by the design and the workmanship.

The introduction of silver had a significant impact on native jewelry. For the Navajo, necklaces evolved from strings of shells and beads to hollow beads of silver interspersed with squash blossom elements and *najas* (crescent-shaped pendants) suspended at the bottom. Waists became adorned with round and oval silver plates strung on leather belts. Not only were new items made for personal adornment, but now clothing and horse trappings could be decorated as well.

1- Photo of Hopi potter Hattie Carl (left) and three young Hopi girls, c. 1910. Carl is wearing a silver squash blossom necklace, and the girls are wearing necklaces made from shell beads.

2- Frasher's postcard entitled "Daughters of Navajo Silversmith," c. 1930. The girls are wearing an abundance of silver jewelry and traditional attire.

3- Turquoise mosaic earrings with abalone shell center inlaid on cottonwood root frames. These are traditional Hopi-style earrings that are worn by young girls and kachinas, especially the Butterfly Maiden (Palhik Mana) Kachina.

The Navajo had acquired a considerable amount of skill at silversmithing by the 1880s, and trade in objects of personal adornment among the various tribes of the area turned into a means of earning a cash income. Navajo silversmiths gained attention from researchers and tourists, and Navajo silver products became souvenirs for Anglos to take "back east."

A Navajo man working silver while the woman on the right uses bellows to keep the fire hot, c. 1900.

Washington Matthews made the first detailed observation of Navajo silversmiths at work and published his findings in the *Second Report of the Bureau of Ethnology for 1880–1881*. Matthews hired a smith—whom he did not name but who was later disclosed to be "Navajo Jake"—to make silver under his scrutiny. Jake lived near Fort Wingate, New Mexico, made and sold silver to the soldiers at the fort, and also worked as a mail carrier. In 1893, Navajo Jake worked for six months demonstrating his craft at the World's Columbian Exposition in Chicago, selling a large quantity of silver to fair visitors; he may well have been the first Navajo to travel off the reservation to work as a silversmith.

In the 1890s, the Fred Harvey Company was purchasing jewelry from traders on the Navajo reservation to sell to travelers along the route of the Atchison, Topeka, and Santa Fe Railway, but this jewelry proved to be too heavy for tourists' tastes. The commercialization of Indian silversmithing began in 1899 when a trader was commissioned to have Navajo silversmiths make lighter weight jewelry with turquoise settings.

At the turn of the twentieth century, the demand for Indian arts and crafts, and Indian jewelry in particular, had grown significantly. George Wharton James wrote in a 1903 newspaper article:

> In the larger eastern cities much interest is now being felt in everything pertaining to the North American Indian. The museums are enlarging their collections, and many ladies are beginning to wear various silver ornaments made by the rude, aboriginal silversmith. Already in New York alone one Navaho silversmith is kept working as many hours as he is capable, and thousands of dollars' worth of silver ornaments are being brought in from the Navaho reservation in New Mexico. The fad is now at its height.

Early earrings: Hopi turquoise mosaic earrings with shell center on cottonwood base, c. 1890, ASM# 3249. Navajo silver squash blossom earrings, c. 1900, ASM# 8265. Pueblo or Navajo silver earrings using recycled turquoise tab pendants, c. 1940, ASM# E-1247. *Courtesy Arizona State Museum, The University of Arizona.*

Merchants soon realized that the presence of an Indian silversmith plying his trade in view of the customers boosted their sales of Indian jewelry. Therefore, following in the footsteps of Navajo Jake, many Navajo, Pueblo, and Hopi silversmiths left home, either on a seasonal or permanent basis, to work in curio stores from Hollywood to New York, or at tourist venues such as the Mohawk Trail in the Northeast, Wisconsin Dells in the Midwest, and Garden of the Gods in Colorado Springs, as well as at national parks such as the Grand Canyon and Zion.

1- John Etsitty, Navajo silversmith at Zion National Park during the 1930s, who preferred to be called John Silversmith. He also worked for Charles Strausenback in Phoenix and at Garden of the Gods Trading Post in Colorado Springs.

2- Collection of early Navajo and Pueblo jewelry, all unmarked except bracelet (left top) with teardrop-shaped turquoise stone, marked SOLID SILVER / HAND MADE AT "THE INDIAN" / GARDEN OF THE GODS COLO. Grouping, c. 1900 to 1930. *Courtesy Madeleine Nash and authors' collection.*

Chapter 2:

THE MANUFACTURERS

By the early twentieth century, at least one business man, Harry Heye Tammen of Denver, Colorado, determined he could mechanize and mass-produce lighter, less expensive silver with Indian-stylized designs that would satisfy not only the souvenir-seeking tourist, but also a larger audience that was intrigued by southwest American Indians. In 1906, the H. H. Tammen Company started a line of Indian-design silver jewelry manufactured with the aid of machinery. The silver shop in Denver, managed by Carl Litzenberger, employed non-Indian workers and operated for at least fifty years, producing a variety of items from jewelry to spoons that utilized pseudo-Indian designs.

1- Unsigned manufactured pins sold by Arrow Novelty Company.

2- Silver bracelet with swastika and arrow designs illustrated in Arrow Novelty Company catalog, c. 1925. Marked with COIN 900 inside an arrowhead.

Carl Litzenberger's brother, Rudolph, was assistant manager of H. H. Tammen in Denver until he moved to New York City and became president of Arrow Novelty Company. About 1925, Arrow published a wholesale catalog of Indian-design silver, and the similarities between Arrow's *Catalogue of Indian Design Silver Jewelry* and a 1908 H. H. Tammen catalog make it evident that Tammen manufactured the jewelry that Arrow sold. Arrow Novelty Company hallmarked only a small amount of their jewelry, usually bracelets, and these were marked with the words COIN 900 imprinted inside an arrowhead.

Maisel's Indian Trading Post brochure, c. 1930.

Then a different approach was taken to create jewelry for the tourist market in the Southwest. Maurice Maisel purchased an Albuquerque music and jewelry store in 1923 across the street from Fred Harvey's Alvarado Hotel. Renaming the business Maisel's Indian Trading Post, he almost immediately started designing a line of jewelry and hired Indian silversmiths to produce it by hand. But the shop could not keep up with the demand, so he began incorporating machinery into the process around 1927. As time went on, the shop was equipped with electric and hand-operated rolling mills, hand- and foot-operated presses, a power hacksaw, and rotary shears, all of which was located at the back of the shop, concealed from public view and operated by Indian workmen. Approximately thirty-five Pueblo and Navajo men worked at Maisel's in 1930 operating machinery and finishing jewelry by hand, and at one time employment peaked at around 165 Indians.

All jewelry items were initially punched out on presses as blanks, and other machines were used to raise elements on the blanks and to punch holes. Indian silversmiths working at long benches, similar to assembly-line production, received the blanks from the presses and then assembled and finished the pieces by stamping, soldering, setting turquoise, and polishing the final product. Many of Maisel's designs were copied from handmade articles.

1- Silver bracelet set with a single row of turquoise manufactured by Maisel's, c. 1940.

2- Copper advertising tray for Maisel's Indian Trading Post, showing kachina-like shop mark with copyright symbol.

3- A rare example of a handmade ring with Maisel's kachina-like shop mark and the words HAND MADE stamped on the underside.

In 1939, Maisel relocated the operation to 510 West Central in Albuquerque, which became the most famous destination in the Southwest for tourists to watch silversmiths at work. An opening in the floor surrounded by a railing allowed visitors to observe the workshop, but they could watch only those silversmiths who hand-finished pieces.

Maisel's utilized a wide variety of hallmarks on its pieces over the years. Some incorporated the name MAISELS with "Sterling;" others used a kachina-like figure with a headdress and a copyright symbol in the skirt. However, a large number of the finished goods produced have no markings of any kind, so it seems Maisel's did not apply hallmarks until the 1940s.

1- Copper arrowhead advertising key fob showing the Bell Trading Post, Inc. shop mark on front side.

2- Nickel silver thunderbird pin with faux turquoise made by Bell Trading Post under their Redskin Maid division. This line of machine-made dime-store jewelry was designed by Wilbert "Blue Sky Eagle" Hunt (Acoma).

3- Handmade cowboy pin (left) by Awa Tsireh (San Ildefonso) while employed at Garden of the Gods Trading Post. A machine-made cowboy pin (right) from Bell Trading Post. Most likely Bell stole this design from Awa Tsireh's handmade pin.

Founded in the early 1930s by Jack Michelson, Bell Trading Post of Albuquerque was a small operation in 1935, with a handful of Pueblo and Navajo silversmiths. Bell's Indian silversmiths made the pieces from sheet silver at shared benches. In 1940, when a foreman was hired to mechanize the operation and make it similar to Maisel's shop, the staff included a dozen Indian silversmiths. The quality of the jewelry that is hallmarked by Bell varies greatly from its earliest pieces, which were fairly well made with genuine turquoise, to later pieces that are inferior with little or no hand finishing and poor or imitation turquoise. Many of Bell's designs were direct copies of handmade Indian silver. In 1947, one of the company's silversmiths, Wilbert Hunt of Acoma, designed a line of copper and nickel silver dime-store jewelry—one dollar would buy three bracelets—that sold under the name "Redskin Maid." Bell remained in business until 1972. The company used two main variations of its hallmark: the earliest is a bell surrounded by the words "sterling," "nickel silver," or "solid copper;" the later marks have a placard imprinted with a bell suspended from an arrow signpost.

Manufactured bracelets sold by the same company under three different business names: Indian Handcrafts, Silver Products, and Silver Arrow.

One business located in Kansas City, Missouri—Silver Products Manufacturing Company—maintained three distinct lines of Indian-design silver that was manufactured by Maisel's. Each different line, Silver Products, Silver Arrow, and Indian Handcrafts, bore its own hallmark. Clues that Maisel's was the source come from a 1943 Silver Products advertising folder that reproduced the exact design symbols from Maisel's brochures and also states, "The fashionable and high quality coin silver jewelry represented by this folder was made in America's largest coin silver and turquoise jewelry factory, employing mostly Indian labor." This description fits Maisel's operation perfectly. The hallmark used on the Silver Products line was an arrow with SILVER PRODUCTS COIN SILVER written above and below the shaft. The mark used on the Silver Arrow line was SILVER ARROW in cursive along a straight arrow with STERLING written in the fletch. The hallmark used for Indian Handcrafts—IH COIN SILVER—was deceptive because it could easily be misconstrued to mean "Indian Handmade." The products displaying these hallmarks are all strictly machine made with little or no hand finishing.

The proliferation of machine-made silver prompted representatives from the Navajo reservation to complain to the Bureau of Indian Affairs in 1929 that imitations were affecting their economy; traditional Indian silversmithing was in decline because traders and silversmiths found it difficult to compete with mass-produced Indian-design jewelry. In 1931, a group of traders formed the United Indian Traders Association (UITA), and one of their goals was to combat the unfair methods of competition used by manufacturers of mass-produced jewelry. The misrepresentation of products in Maisel's catalogs was brought to the attention of the Federal Trade Commission (FTC). The FTC instituted proceedings against Maisel's in 1932, focusing on its use of the slogan "Indian Made Jewelry;" the complaint charged that the products were not those of handcraft or artistry. Maurice Maisel denied the allegations, maintaining that his Albuquerque workshop was not a factory, that he employed only full-blooded Indians, and that those Indians produced all of the jewelry the company made and sold.

Advertising brochures for Indian Handcrafts and Silver Products, distributors of Indian-design silver jewelry based in Kansas City, Missouri.

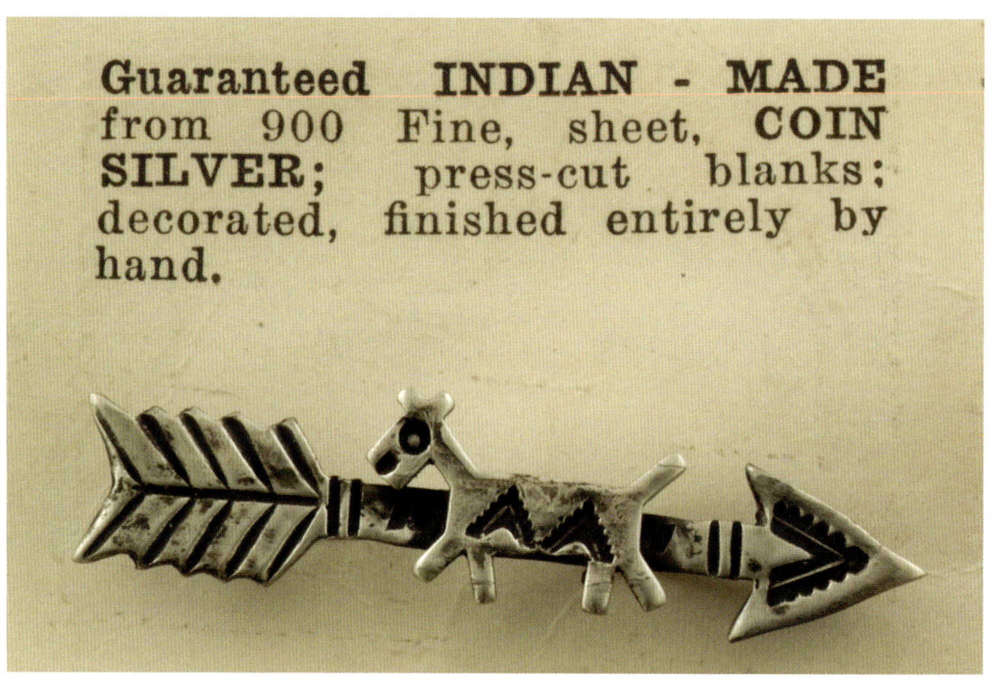

Arrow pin with dog appliqué on original display card manufactured by Maisel's, c. 1935.

The FTC ordered Maisel's to cease and desist in 1933 from using the terms "Indian" or "Indian-made" unless it clearly specified that the products were the result of machine processing. Maisel fought against the FTC until 1936, when it was ruled that he met the requirements by affixing labeling to the products denoting manufacturing methods; for example, "Guaranteed Indian-Made from 900 Fine, sheet, Coin Silver; press-cut blanks; decorated, finished entirely by hand."

Despite the FTC ruling, Maisel's continued its deceptive practices. Later advertising folders stated, "Our Indian Trading Post at Albuquerque is manned by silversmiths from both the Navajo and Pueblo tribes and all of our jewelry is made by these Indians. No white man makes or finishes any part of it," and then detailed how the workers used rollers, presses, or drop hammer "to prepare the silver for the hand work."

In the end, no matter what the FTC, the federal government, or the UITA tried to do to curtail machine-made jewelry from dominating the market, it was useless. Maisel's and Bell were successful operations simply because their jewelry was more affordable and its appearance was more "authentic" to the average tourist who wanted little more than an inexpensive souvenir to take back home. Today Indian-design jewelry mass-produced by the mechanized shops and factories is often termed "Fred Harvey era jewelry."

The Swastika Symbol

One of the most popular jewelry designs used for the curio trade was the swastika symbol, common to most indigenous peoples the world over and used throughout time. There is historical precedence of the use of swastika-like designs by North American native peoples, who usually viewed the symbol as a representation of the four directions: the Navajo use a design often referred to as "whirling logs" in sandpaintings, and the Hopi paint a four-armed pinwheel design on rattles symbolizing the migrations of the clans across the continent.

A great deal of interest was generated about the swastika symbol around the turn of the twentieth century. In North America, it became a very popular design element symbolizing good luck and was prevalent in period architecture, advertising, jewelry, and on good luck tokens. Because of its popularity, traders encouraged Indian artists to use it on their crafts made for the tourist trade from about 1890 to 1940. The design often appeared on silverwork as well as textiles, pottery, and basketry.

Starting in 1934, East Coast dealers of Indian goods urged traders to discourage craftspeople from using the swastika as a design element on Indian arts and crafts because of its adoption by the German Nazi Party. Popularity of the design waned in the following years, eventually resulting in a proclamation signed on February 28, 1940, in Tucson by representatives from the Hopi, Navajo, Apache, and Tohono O'odham (formerly Papago) tribes, renouncing and banning the use of the swastika on their artwork:

> Because the above ornament which has been a symbol of friendship among our forefathers for many centuries has been desecrated recently by another nation of peoples,
>
> Therefore it is resolved that henceforth from this date on and forever more our tribes renounce the use of the emblem commonly known today as the swastika or fylfot on our blankets, baskets, art objects, sandpaintings and clothing.

1- Copper bookends by Morris Robinson (Hopi). The swastika design indicates they were made before 1940.

2- Postcard showing Indians from various southwest tribes signing a declaration that they would not use the swastika symbol on their artwork after February 28, 1940.

Chapter 3:

The Traders

The best known and most influential "trader" of Indian jewelry was the Fred Harvey Company. Founded in 1876 in Topeka, Kansas, the company built and managed eating establishments and hotels located along the tracks of the Atchison, Topeka, and Santa Fe Railway from Kansas to California. The Harvey Company established the Indian Department—headquartered at the Alvarado Hotel in Albuquerque—in 1902 as a museum and showroom to promote and to sell Indian handmade goods in its lodges, shops, and restaurants. By the first decade of the twentieth century, the Fred Harvey Company had become the largest distributor of high-quality Indian arts in the United States, shipping boxcar loads of arts and crafts to eastern markets.

In 1899, Herman Schweizer, who would later manage the Indian Department, commissioned a turquoise mine to pre-cut and polish stones in various shapes. He then asked traders around Gallup, New Mexico, to commission Navajo smiths to make jewelry using lighter weight silver and the stones he provided. As the business grew, Schweizer would purchase finished silver mostly from New Mexico traders: Crown Point Trading Company and L. C. Smith in Thoreau, Gallup Mercantile and Kirk Brothers in Gallup, and Kelsey Trading Company and C. G. Wallace at Zuni.

1- Heavy copper, hand-hammered, cowboy hat ashtray made exclusively for Fred Harvey Company, c. 1935. Their 1938 catalog implied these hats were not made by Indians; the description stated only that they were hand-hammered. Prices ranged from 50¢ to $1.50 depending on size.

2- This spoon, engraved "1914 Grand Canon of the Colorado, Made by the Hopi Indians," is an early verified piece made by a Hopi silversmith. The Harvey Company employed Hopi and Navajo silversmiths in the Hopi House at the Grand Canyon across from El Tovar Hotel. *Courtesy Karen Sires.*

Schweizer and the Harvey Company quickly discovered their sales of Indian jewelry increased significantly at the Alvarado Hotel when tourists could observe an Indian silversmith hammering out jewelry. In 1902 hogans were built near the Alvarado to house Navajo silversmiths and their wives; the latter were employed to demonstrate rug weaving. Also, when the Hopi House opened at the Grand Canyon in 1905 the Harvey Company employed Navajo and Hopi silversmiths there.

While the Harvey Company became a major buyer of Indian jewelry in the Gallup area, other traders catered to supplying East Coast buyers, and Gallup soon became the hub of handmade Indian jewelry production.

John Lorenzo Hubbell, trader at Ganado, Arizona, was the first reservation trader to offer Navajo handmade silver by mail order in his 1902 catalog. In 1903 the trader at Crystal, New Mexico, J. B. Moore, was promoting Navajo silver to eastern customers by including three pages of silverwork in his mail order catalog. Items for sale included squash blossom necklaces, souvenir spoons, rings, stick pins, bridles, bracelets, and silver belts. In 1906 Navajo silver became a larger part of Moore's business, and he published a separate eight-page pamphlet, *Illustrated Catalogue of Navajo Hand-Made Silverwork*, in which he stated, "All my goods are made from coin silver furnished my own silversmiths, and I keep two of the most expert known to me constantly employed."

J. H. (Joel Higgins) McAdams ran numerous trading posts on the Navajo reservation from 1898 to 1910. Afterwards he established McAdams Trading Company in Gallup, where he dealt exclusively in Indian jewelry and trained Navajo silversmiths to make fancy, lightweight silver. He advertised widely in eastern newspapers and had success with mail orders, so that he was able to employ and train more silversmiths. He claimed that during his time in business thousands of Navajo silversmiths learned their trade in the shop behind his store. McAdams sold his company to John Kirk in 1918 and was occupied with other business ventures until his death in 1929.

Silversmithing began to be commercialized at Zuni Pueblo in the early 1900s through the influence of traders who were filling orders for the Fred Harvey Company. Charles Kelsey started trading at Zuni in 1906 and worked to develop production and markets.

C. G. Wallace (far right) in front of his Zuni trading post, 1957.

C. G. WALLACE INDIAN ARTS & CRAFTS

ESTABLISHED 1928

104 E. 66 AVE. — GALLUP, NEW MEXICO

DISTINCTIVE ZUNI AND NAVAJO HANDICRAFT

JEWELRY -:- RUGS -:- POTTERY -:- BEADWORK

WHOLESALE AND RETAIL : : GENUINE RESERVATION HANDMADE

RESERVATION TRADING POSTS

C. G. WALLACE, ZUNI, N. MEX.

RANCHERS SUPPLY, SANDERS, ARIZ.

CEDAR POINT TRADING POST
SANDERS, ARIZONA

Business card for C. G. Wallace, c. 1940. The Gallup retail and wholesale outlet was opened in 1928.

C. G. (Charles Garrett) Wallace came to New Mexico in 1918 and shortly after was hired by Louis Ilfeld. He worked at Ramah on the Navajo reservation and for Charles Kelsey at Zuni. Wallace later applied for a license to operate his own trading post, and in 1928 opened a store in Zuni. A second trading post at Cedar Point, Arizona, where Wallace traded with the Navajo, was also acquired.

1- Unsigned inlaid pin by Lambert Homer Sr. (Zuni), c. 1930, inlaid with Blue Gem turquoise. This pin was purchased from C. G. Wallace's personal collection. *Courtesy Madeleine Nash.*

2- Navajo silver table boxes, 1930–1940. Left box marked with flower hallmark is attributed to Joe Yazzie (Navajo). Right box with Zuni Knifewing inlay is unsigned. Both boxes made by Navajo smiths working in the Zuni area.

3- Silver boxes, c. 1930. Center front marked with tomahawk, possibly by Austin Wilson (Navajo); far right marked with arching arrow, by unknown Navajo silversmith who worked for C. G. Wallace; oval box and match box are unmarked.

C. G. Wallace is well known for his promotion of, and influence on, Zuni jewelry. From the 1930s into the 1950s, he actively bought and sold silverwork from the Zuni and the Navajo residing in the area. Wallace sold the Zuni trading post in 1958 while continuing to operate the Cedar Point trading post. Though Wallace never developed a shop mark for silver made at his trading posts, many silversmiths who worked for him used some sort of personal hallmark, a number of which have yet to be identified. Wallace was known to purchase lapidary-cut settings from the Zuni and then to consign them to Navajo silversmiths who inlaid the settings in silver; these smiths sometimes placed their hallmark on the finished pieces.

Handmade silver and copper tourist items, 1930s–1940s, all unmarked as to metal content, shop, or individual maker, except dog fob (far right) marked by Morris Robinson (Hopi).

Mike Kirk, the trader at Manuelito, New Mexico, told John Adair, author of *Navajo and Pueblo Silversmiths*, that his business had expanded rapidly from the time he started dealing in silver about 1910. At that time, only two Navajo silversmiths resided near him who could produce decent silverwork. But in the late 1930s, more than one hundred smiths worked under his supervision, and that did not include the smiths who did freelance work. Adair, in his book, noted that most of the items commissioned by Kirk were novelties in the forms of butterflies, lizards, goat heads, and bucking horses.

About 1925, Berton I. Staples began construction of a trading post that he would call Crafts del Navajo at Coolidge, New Mexico, located about twenty miles east of Gallup on Route 66. Attached to the trading post was Casa del Navajo, which included living quarters, a museum, and rooms for visitors; it was promoted as an oasis of culture in the southwest desert. On the property were several hogans where Navajo silversmiths and weavers created their crafts for tourists and visitors to observe. To capitalize on the fascination of American Indians by eastern residents, Staples organized a three-month-long tour in 1930 stopping at museums, schools, organizations, and retail outlets through twenty-three states in cities ranging from New York to Washington, D.C., and Chicago. Navajo participants included a silversmith, a weaver, and a sandpainter; while Staples gave presentations about Navajo arts and crafts, the craftspeople would demonstrate their skills. Tours continued every winter and featured Da-Pah as the silversmith; he and his wife, a weaver, lived and worked at Crafts del Navajo when they were not on tour. Staples was killed in an automobile accident on October 9, 1938, and the trading post was purchased by Charlie Newcomb soon after Staples's death.

1- Four handmade copper trays, unmarked except bottom left that is marked HAND MADE BY INDIANS, indicating it was made at Garden of the Gods Trading Post. Copper was a very popular medium from the 1920s to the 1950s.

2- Copper table boxes, c. 1930. Left box includes appliquéd thunderbird on lid and three turquoise settings. The box appears to be handmade, but the thunderbird may have been cut out by machine. Right box is completely handmade with a repoussé button design on the lid.

1

2

Most traders in Arizona and New Mexico had at least one silversmith supplying them with silver, often living with his family at, or in close proximity to, the trading post. Wick Miller, a trader located in San Ysidro, New Mexico—halfway between the pueblos of Zia and Jemez—had two Navajo silversmiths living on site making silver and copper items to be sold through his trading post in 1931.

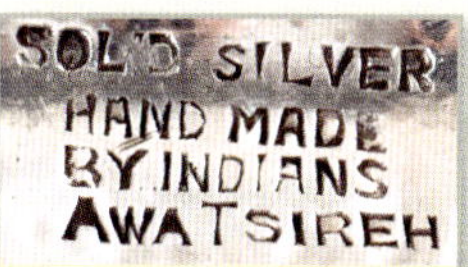

Two pins made between 1941 and 1945 in the shape of a "V" signifying "V for Victory" during World War II. The Zuni pin (left) has three dots and a dash at the bottom, Morse code for the letter "V"; the pin (right) by Awa Tsireh utilizes doves to form the V.

Silversmithing became a good means for Indian craftsmen to earn a living, and most of them gravitated to the Gallup area in the 1930s where, within a fifty-mile radius, most Indian silver was being made. The silver industry became big business, and in 1946, after the end of the Second World War, approximately $10 million worth of Indian jewelry was sold.

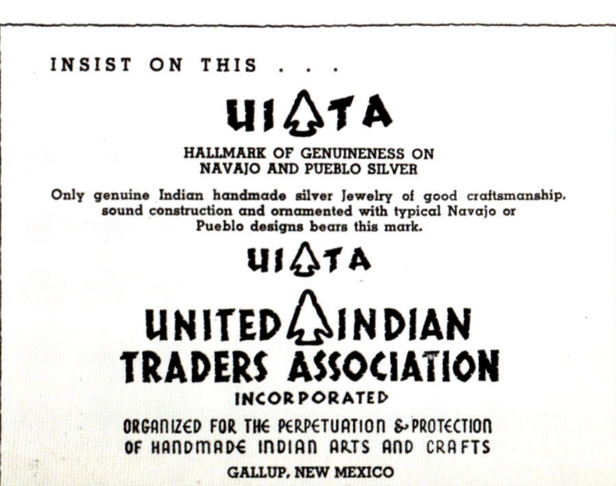
INSIST ON THIS . . .

UITA

HALLMARK OF GENUINENESS ON NAVAJO AND PUEBLO SILVER

Only genuine Indian handmade silver Jewelry of good craftsmanship, sound construction and ornamented with typical Navajo or Pueblo designs bears this mark.

UITA

UNITED INDIAN TRADERS ASSOCIATION

INCORPORATED

ORGANIZED FOR THE PERPETUATION & PROTECTION OF HANDMADE INDIAN ARTS AND CRAFTS

GALLUP, NEW MEXICO

Advertisement placed in a 1946 magazine announcing the United Indian Traders Association hallmark program.

United Indian Traders Association

Berton Staples and other Indian traders concerned with the proliferation of imitation Indian crafts, specifically jewelry, met in August 1931, after the Gallup Inter-Tribal Ceremonial. To better organize their efforts in combating manufacturers like Maisel's, they formed the United Indian Traders Association (UITA). Staples was elected president and the other officers were R. C. Master of Zuni and Tobe Turpen and C. N. Cotton, both of Gallup. Seven directors were elected including Lew Sabin, Fort Defiance; C. G. Wallace, Zuni; J. M. Drolet, Naschitti (Tohatchi); Roman Hubbell, Ganado; Lloyd Ambrose, Thoreau; Bruce M. Barnard, Shiprock; and Mike Kirk, Manuelito. There were seventy-five charter members, and most of them were traders from the Navajo reservation. Membership grew to include arts and crafts dealers in areas removed from the reservations, including, in 1934, Charles Strausenback, owner of Garden of the Gods Trading Post in Colorado Springs.

Butterfly, thunderbird, and owl pins, all with UITA hallmarks. Top row (left to right): UITA5, UITA6, UITA21. Middle row: UITA3, UITA22, UITA3. Bottom row: UITA22, UITA3, UITA5.

The new organization's stated goals were to promote, to encourage, and to protect the manufacture and sale of genuine Indian handmade arts and crafts, as well as to improve business practices among traders and dealers. For the first few years, the main interest of the association was the unfair competition by manufacturers of imitation Indian crafts, and they were instrumental in obtaining a ban on the sale of such imitations in all national park concessions.

Six pins. Top row (left to right): UITA17, flower pin UITA21, moss agate pin UITA19. Bottom row: horse UITA22, concho UITA22, deer UITA5.

By 1943, membership had grown to about 125 traders and dealers located in several states. At a meeting in December, a committee of eight members, each one highly knowledgeable in Indian jewelry, was formed to study plans for improvement of the handmade Indian jewelry industry. Committee members were Al Frick of Gross Kelly Company, C. G. Wallace and George Rummage from Zuni, Dan Christensen at Pinedale, Dean Kirk of Manuelito, Noble Milam of Gallup Mercantile, John Kirk Jr. of Gallup, and J. M. Drolet.

1

2

1- UITA paper barbell tag used to mark jewelry, such as rings, that could not be stamped with a die. This tag was made for Packard's in Santa Fe.

2- Copper concho belt UITA21, barrette UITA12, pill box UITA26, spoon UITA21, buttons UITA22.

Years of work by the UITA culminated on March 22, 1946, when the association announced its silver stamping program in a press release that appeared in many newspapers and magazines. A General Bulletin sent to members outlined the program: UITA members wishing to use the stamp would be licensed and bonded, and only those members who had a reasonably close control, direct or indirect, over the production of Navajo and Pueblo silver objects would be licensed. Included with the license would be two steel die stamps, one straight and one curved, each bearing a number designating the licensed member, and five thousand printed paper tags. The General Bulletin included a list of standards and regulations for "Genuine Navajo and Pueblo Hand-Made Silver Jewelry."

Silver bracelet with Pueblo design marked UITA 22. *Courtesy Karen Sires.*

The standards stated that the stamp was to be affixed only to work individually produced and entirely handmade, and the design elements of the work were required to be typically Navajo or Pueblo. No object produced under conditions resembling a benchwork system or made with the use of power-driven machinery, except for buffing and polishing, would be eligible. Items must have been made using coin or sterling silver in the form of slugs or sheets. Turquoise and other stones must be genuine and untreated, but could be cut and polished with no restrictions to the equipment used. Casting was permissible using sandstone molds that were entirely hand carved by an Indian.

Salt and pepper shakers UITA12, top bracelet UITA6 with Fred Thompson hallmark as design element, lower bracelet UITA15, buckle UITA2. *Courtesy Robert F. Farling.*

These standards applied only to silver objects, but inexplicably some pieces made from copper also bear the stamp. The General Bulletin of 1946 specified that numbers would be assigned to individual members who were bonded and licensed; numbers were not assigned to businesses or trading posts. The records for the UITA silver stamping program have been lost, though Barton Wright and Tom Woodard, son of M. L. Woodard, initiated the task of reconstructing the list of assigned numbers. Other attempts have been made at rebuilding the list, but many numbers have been attributed by guesswork and word of mouth. For instance, number 3 has been attributed to Berton Staples at Coolidge, but he passed away in 1938 and could not have been bonded in 1946 when the UITA silver program was initiated. A few numbers, however, can be confirmed from various sources: number 2 belonged to C. G. Wallace at Zuni, number 6 to Don Smouse at Borrego Pass, number 12 to Packard's in Santa Fe, number 21 to Julius Gans of Southwest Arts and Crafts in Santa Fe, and number 24 to the owner or manager of Wide Ruins Trading Post. Other attributions can be inferred, such as number 22 to Dean Kirk of Manuelito. With existing information at hand, it cannot be known conclusively which numbers were assigned to which members; perhaps more research will unearth a helpful document at some future date.

Cast Knifewing pin made for C. G. Wallace, attributed to Horace Iule (Zuni), marked UITA2. *Courtesy Karen Sires.*

A 1951 article by M. L. Woodard in the *Gallup Independent* newspaper hinted at the traders who likely had UITA numbers. At Zuni, there were C. G. Wallace and Mrs. C. H. Kelsey (who was running the business her late husband started decades earlier). Don Smouse at Borrego Pass "continually employs a string of silversmiths," and his post had become well known for its table silver. Charles McGee near Thoreau and Dean Kirk and John P. Wall (who purchased Mike Kirk's post after his death in 1942) in Manuelito were prominent traders in Navajo silver. Dan Christensen "put Pinedale on the map in the making of silver beads," and "Stewart Thompson continues the fine traditions of sand-cast jewelry at Pine Springs." In the Gallup area were the Kirk Brothers, Gallup Mercantile Company (likely under their subsidiary Gallup Indian Jewelry), and the Tobe Turpen family. South of Gallup, the Cousins brothers and the Vander Waggen brothers were known for their silver output, and on the west side of the Navajo reservation, Babbitt Brothers was a prominent dealer of silver. Not mentioned in the Woodard article, but noted elsewhere as significant silver traders, were J. M. Drolet of Naschitti, who sold his post in 1950; Roman Hubbell of Ganado; Claude Bowlin of Old Crater Trading Post, east of Gallup, who stated that he "sold only UITA silverwork in his stores"; and possibly Harold Prewitt at Prewitt, New Mexico.

Membership in the UITA in 1950 had grown to include some three hundred traders on the Navajo, Zuni, and Hopi reservations as well as dealers spread throughout the country. The silver stamping program seems to have been successful because the volume of pieces still on the market bearing the UITA stamp outnumbers all other shop marks used in the same period.

It is unknown how long the silver stamping program was enforced, but, in 1966, M. L. Woodard related to Margery Bedinger that the United Indian Traders Association at that time did little in craft work or promotion, and "its licensed mark is rarely if ever used." Nor is it known what became of the approximately forty individually numbered die stamps that were produced for the program. Silver could have been marked without supervision for decades before and after the UITA officially dissolved the association in the late 1990s.

Hallmarks used by United Indian Traders Association members.

Chapter 4:

THE SHOPS

To identify silver handmade by Indian silversmiths working on the premises of their curio shops, some owners created hallmarks that were applied to the jewelry made under their supervision. When these "shop marks" were applied to finished pieces, the silversmiths often did not include their own personal hallmark.

Some shops were located on reservations, such as The Tewa at Isleta Pueblo owned by Diego Abeita. And even though Babbitt Brothers owned trading posts on the Navajo reservation, the company also had a workshop in the Flagstaff retail store that employed at least three Navajo silversmiths in the 1930s. Shops were common from the 1920s through the 1980s in many areas of the Southwest.

1- Three Navajo silversmiths are shown working at Babbitt's Indian Shop in Flagstaff in this late 1930s postcard. It is possible Kenneth Begay and Allen Kee are two of the silversmiths in this photo, as both were employed in the shop around this time.

2- Right pin marked STERLING HAND MADE, possibly a shop mark used by Southwest Arts and Crafts. Center, HAND MADE HOPI pin and HAND MADE NAVAJO pendant made for unknown shop. Left pin, unmarked, using Hopi Guild design, made by Navajo smith working at Woodard's in Gallup.

3- Inlaid buckle marked HAND MADE ZUNI, made for the same unknown shop as pieces marked HAND MADE HOPI and HAND MADE NAVAJO.

1- "The Tewa," c. 1935. Located in Isleta Pueblo and owned by Isleta silversmith Diego Abeita, who employed experienced silversmiths from the village and encouraged them to make traditional-style jewelry. The shop was equipped with modern tools, and the silver produced was of good design and quality.

2- Modern-design hair combs, c. 1950, marked with "W" for Woodard's Indian Arts in Gallup and IHM S/S for Indian Hand Made Sterling Silver. *Courtesy Pam Evans/Shonto Canyon.*

3- Modern-design bracelet, early 1980s, made by Philbert Poseyesva (Hopi) while he worked for Shades of the West shop in Scottsdale. Poseyesva learned silversmithing at Hopicrafts.

1

2

3

Garden of the Gods Trading Post

In the early 1900s, Colorado Springs was a popular starting place to see the many tourist attractions in the Pike's Peak region of Colorado. North of the city was a public park called the Garden of the Gods that contained unusual sandstone formations. Charles E. Strausenback started in business by selling curios to tourists at the park.

Strausenback was born in 1890 and, at the age of twenty-three, was employed by the Fred Harvey Company at the newsstand in the Alvarado Hotel. Close proximity to the Harvey Indian Department introduced him to Indian arts and crafts, and, before 1917, Strausenback had relocated to Colorado Springs and was married and self-employed in a curio business at the gateway to the Garden of the Gods. By May 1920, Garden of the Gods Curio Company was established in a wood building, which Strausenback had acquired from a previous owner, at the south entrance to the park.

Navajo and Pueblo Indians were hired to work at the curio store, making crafts and entertaining the tourists. Two of the earliest silversmiths to work for Strausenback were from Santa Clara Pueblo, Epifanio Tafoya and his nephew Severo Tafoya, who were hired about 1925.

1

SEE THE PETRIFIED INDIAN (CLIFF DWELLER) FREE
AT "THE INDIAN"
GARDEN OF THE GODS CURIO CO.
GARDEN OF THE GODS CURIO CO.
GARDEN OF THE GODS, COLORADO
Hyland 106-J
CHAS. E. STRAUSENBACK
P. O. BOX 686
COLORADO SPRINGS

1- 1927 business card for Garden of the Gods Curio Company; at that time the trading post was called "The Indian."

2

2- The first known version of Garden of the Gods Curio Company, in a photo taken May 3, 1920. The sign on top of the wood structure reads, "See the Petrified Indian Inside."

3

3- Photo postcard of Epifanio Tafoya (Santa Clara) working silver at Garden of the Gods Curio Company, c. 1925. His Indian name was Na-Na-Ping (1879–1933).

1- Photo of Strausenback's trading post, 1926. This newly constructed stone masonry building displays a sign over the left entrance proclaiming its name as "The Indian."

2- Six bracelets, all c. 1925, marked SOLID SILVER HAND MADE AT THE "INDIAN" GARDEN OF THE GODS – COLO. The turquoise stones are cut and polished by hand. They could have been made by William Goodluck (Navajo), Epifanio Tafoya, or Severo Tafoya (both of Santa Clara Pueblo).

Plans were made to build a Pueblo-themed structure to house an Indian curio museum and trading post. The structure was erected in 1926 and named "The Indian;" included on the grounds were a Pueblo-styled kiva and a Navajo hogan. Silver made at the trading post from about 1925 to 1930 was marked SOLID SILVER HAND MADE AT THE "INDIAN" GARDEN OF THE GODS-COLO. The majority of the pieces made were bracelets with typical tourist-type figural designs including thunderbirds, swastikas, arrows, and squash blossoms stamped on hand-hammered ingot coin silver. Most items were heavy plain silver, but a few pieces received settings of turquoise that were cut and polished by hand.

About 1930, the name "The Indian" was retired, the building became known as Garden of the Gods Trading Post, and the business name was changed to Garden of the Gods Trading Company. At this time, Strausenback incorporated a logo that would become synonymous with his business. Painted on the front of his trading post, used on his business card, and made into shop mark dies was the image of a Tewa thunderbird and coiled snake drawn by San Ildefonso artist Awa Tsireh (Alfonso Roybal). Strausenback had the logo copyrighted about 1930. Awa Tsireh also worked for Strausenback as a silversmith from about 1930 to the late 1940s.

1- Late 1930s postcard of Garden of the Gods Trading Post. A sign states, "Free See The Indian Silversmiths," and the business was advertised as "the only trading post in Colorado where you can see the Navajos and Pueblo Indians, making silver jewelry."

2- Garden of the Gods Trading Post postcard, c. 1930. Severo and Porfillia Tafoya are on far left; in the center is William Goodluck working at a stump while his family sits nearby. Logo on portico adapted from a painting by Awa Tsireh depicts Tewa Thunderbird and snake.

CHAS. E. STRAUSENBACK INDIAN TRADER
Mail Address Post Office Box 686 Colorado Springs, Colorado

INDIAN SILVER SHOPS

GARDEN OF THE GODS TRADING COMPANY
©
Est. 1900

INDIAN TRADING POST
Garden of the Gods, Colorado
Phone Hyland 48

ANTLERS INDIAN SHOP
Antlers Hotel, Colorado Springs
Phone Main 1200

STRAUSENBACK'S INDIAN SILVER SHOPS
105 North Central Ave.
Phoenix, Arizona

3- Charles Strausenback's business card, c. 1940. He owned Garden of the Gods Trading Post and also ran an Indian curio shop in the Antlers Hotel, a separate silver shop in Phoenix, and a gift shop in the Adams Hotel, Phoenix, not mentioned on the card.

1- Early 1930s copper dish with thunderbird and swastika stamps, and a silver Pueblo design thunderbird pendant on handmade chain, both made at Garden of the Gods Trading Post.

2- Two bracelets, one copper, one silver; buttons and pill box; all made at Garden of the Gods Trading Post by unidentified silversmiths.

Many articles of silver, nickel silver, and copper were produced by the Indians who worked for Strausenback, from wearable jewelry to curios, boxes, table ware, and flatware. The design stamps gradually moved from figural tourist designs to simpler design elements combined in artistic ways to produce an overall elegant effect. This change was a reflection of the style Awa Tsireh used to decorate his metalwork. The Tewa thunderbird logo, minus the snake, was made into two versions of shop stamps used on some of the metalwork made in the workshop. The other shop marks used by Strausenback were SOLID SILVER or STERLING and HAND MADE BY INDIANS; only the SOLID SILVER stamp was used before and after the name of the business changed from "The Indian."

1- Photo postcard of Severo Tafoya (or Ca-Ping, Santa Clara, 1906–1985), shown working at Garden of the Gods Curio Company, c. 1925.

Severo Tafoya (Ca-Ping) from Santa Clara worked for Strausenback for decades, he and his wife Porfillia (Ja-Ro) were photographed often for advertising postcards. Severo and Porfillia made a permanent home in Colorado Springs, and that is where Severo died at the age of 79 in 1985. He did not use a personal hallmark, so it is impossible to identify his work.

2- Copper plate (6" dia.), marked with the Garden of the Gods Tewa Thunderbird shop mark. The Pueblo-style thundercloud design and artistic workmanship suggest it was made by a Pueblo smith who studied with Awa Tsireh, likely Ca-Ping (Severo Tafoya).

Another silversmith to work for Strausenback at this time, 1927 if not sooner, was William "Billy" Goodluck (Navajo), son of renowned silversmith Hosteen Goodluck. William, born about 1891, was from Lupton, Arizona, and worked for Strausenback seasonally for many years, bringing his family with him to the Garden of the Gods. Early postcards of Goodluck identify him as "Host-Nat-Woty." Goodluck also did not incorporate a personal hallmark, but his work can sometimes be attributed by the style of fabrication.

In 1936, John Silversmith (Navajo), whose name was actually John Etsitty, worked for Strausenback in Phoenix, and in 1938 at the trading post in Colorado Springs. Also in 1938, Ralph (Rafael) Roybal (San Ildefonso), the younger brother of Awa Tsireh, worked as a silversmith at Garden of the Gods Trading Co. In 1955, Melvin Johnnie, who was more than likely Navajo, and Antonio Duran, from Picuris Pueblo, were probably the last silversmiths employed at the trading post.

1- Postcard postmarked July 16, 1927. Written on back, "We stopped this morning at the Garden of the Gods and there I met William Goodluck. ... He is a silversmith (Navajo). ... He gave me this picture to send you." Front of card provides his tribal name "Host-Nat-Woty."

2- William Goodluck (Navajo) and family on porch of Garden of the Gods Trading Post, c. 1930 postcard.

There were many other silversmiths who worked for Strausenback over the years, but only a few signed their work. A few pieces by David Taliman (Navajo) have surfaced that are signed with his personal mark D. TALIMAN and SOLID SILVER HAND MADE BY INDIANS, but it is unknown when he worked for Strausenback. And other pieces with Garden of the Gods shop marks also include personal hallmarks, but the artists remain unidentified.

Strausenback passed away around 1956 in Colorado Springs, and his wife Esther continued to run the business. The trading post was purchased by T. A. T. Enterprises in 1979, which operates it as a combination gift shop, Indian art gallery, café, conference center, and wedding venue. The tools used by the silversmiths are displayed in a case in the trading post.

Silver bracelet with agate settings made at Garden of the Gods Trading Post. Marked BA with kachina-like figure, SOLID SILVER and HAND MADE BY INDIANS, by artist as yet unknown.

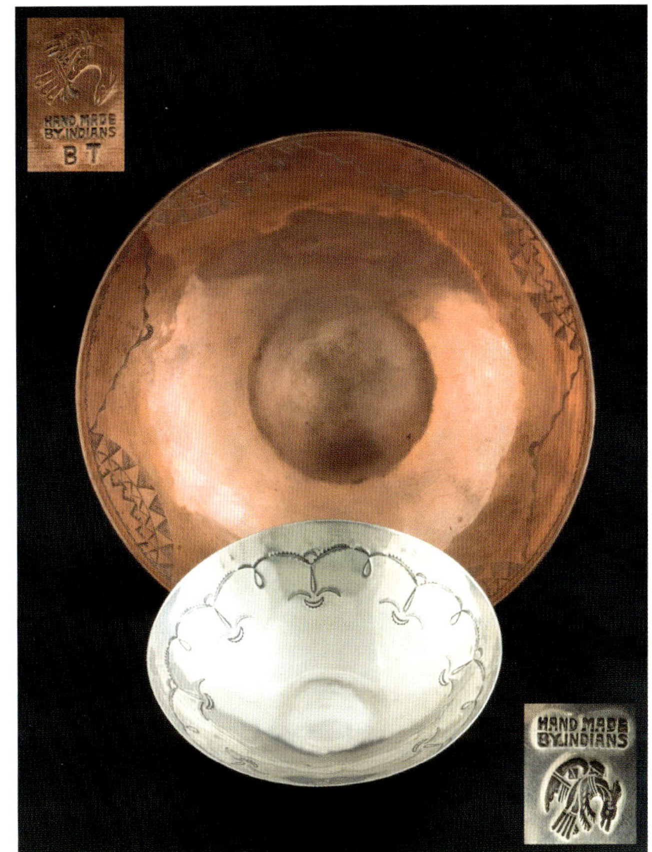

Silver and copper bowls made at Garden of the Gods Trading Post, both marked with HAND MADE BY INDIANS and Tewa Thunderbird shop marks; copper bowl (8.5" dia.) also includes the initials BT in the hallmark, artist as yet unidentified.

Southwest Arts and Crafts

Julius Gans moved to Santa Fe in 1915 and opened a curio store on the plaza. Named Southwest Arts and Crafts (SWAC), it was to become the largest retail curio business in Santa Fe. Gans designed his own line of handmade Indian silver in 1927, hiring Navajo and Pueblo silversmiths to make the jewelry in a workshop visible from the retail sales floor. The shop utilized sheet silver and the best turquoise available; it had two rows of benches with twenty-four positions, and each silversmith made one piece at a time from start to finish.

1- Business card for Southwest Arts and Crafts, c. 1920.

2- Claudio Perez of Nambe Pueblo making a silver bracelet at Southwest Arts and Crafts in Santa Fe, New Mexico, c. 1935. Postcard published by Frasher's.

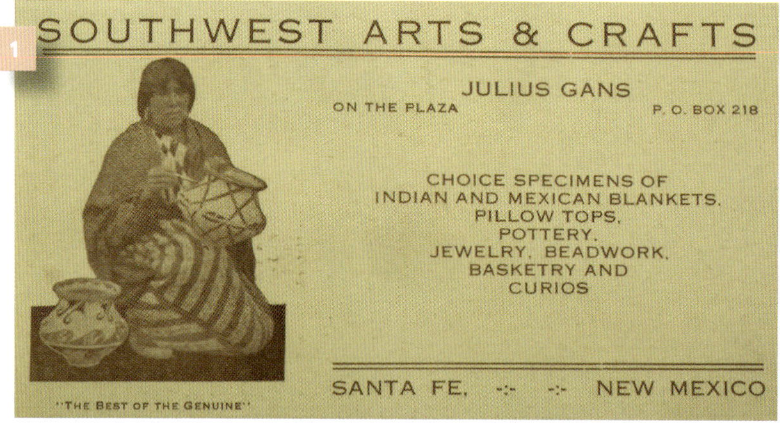

Gans employed many smiths who would go on to become well known, including Ambrose Roanhorse, David Taliman, Mark Chee (Navajo), and Joe Quintana of Cochiti. Around 1938 Gans initiated a system where smiths could work at home; they were given a work order, the necessary template, and the silver and turquoise required. In 1940, fifteen of twenty-five smiths employed by SWAC, including Joe Quintana, worked from their homes. The workshop attached to the retail store continued to operate until 1941 when it was dismantled; afterward, all silver was made in silversmith's homes.

Gans's business was complicated by the FTC's decision against Maisel's in 1933. Even though Gans's operation was more reputable, it was grouped by the government into the same category as Maisel's simply because his smiths used sheet silver as a labor-saving device and they sat at common work benches that resembled Maisel's assembly-line production.

After the Maisel's ruling, the UITA took action to stop the sale of imitation Indian arts and crafts in the national parks. Secretary of the Interior Harold Ickes ruled that only handmade Indian jewelry was to be sold in national park gift shops. Gans assured his buyers that his products met the qualifications of genuine Indian handmade silver. But in May 1935, the Harvey Company, for which Gans had been a major supplier, removed SWAC silver from sale at the Grand Canyon and stopped buying jewelry from Gans altogether. Other concessionaires were told by the National Park Service to cease selling SWAC products. After further investigation, Ickes formally banned SWAC from selling to national park concessions because sheet silver was used in its products.

Pins handmade for Southwest Arts and Craft and marked with an "S" on back to designate the use of slug silver. A 1930s law stated all Indian jewelry sold in the National Park system had to be hand-hammered from slug silver; no sheet silver could be used.

To regain the largest part of his business, Gans found it necessary to purchase one-ounce slugs of coin silver to make products for sale in the national parks. The jewelry made by Gans's smiths at home in the pueblos was sold to the parks; these pieces were marked with an "S" to denote the use of slug silver. The only other shop mark used by Gans was UITA21 after 1946 as a participant in the United Indian Traders Association silver stamping program.

Thunderbird pin handmade at Seligman's in Albuquerque, New Mexico, c. 1940, and marked on back INDIAN HAND MADE STERLING. *Private collection.*

Seligman's

In the 1930s, Bernalillo Mercantile Company, owned by Julius and Siegfried Seligman, introduced a line of silver jewelry designed by Siegfried. Employing mostly Navajo silversmiths, the shop utilized no machinery except electric buffers, and each smith sat at his own workbench. The finished pieces were affixed with a keyhole-shaped adhesive tag reading, "Genuine Indian Jewelry Handmade from Sterling Silver by the Navaho Indians." In 1946, Julius moved to Albuquerque and opened a retail shop and workshop that he named Seligman's. He employed two Navajo silversmiths and built hogans behind the shop so they could live on the property. In 1959, Seligman's added punch presses and tumblers for polishing, and Joe Quintana joined the business as a designer. Seligman's used INDIAN HAND MADE as a shop mark with the word "Indian" arched over "Hand Made."

Vaughn's Indian Store

Reese Vaughn came to Phoenix in 1900, bought an established curio shop in 1918, and operated it as Vaughn's Indian Store. He built and expanded the business until it was "Arizona's largest curio store" in the early 1930s. At one point, five Indian silversmiths were employed, including at various times Fred Peshlakai (Navajo) and Ralph Tawangyawma, Morris Robinson, and Paul Saufkie (Hopi).

After selling the Phoenix store in 1936, Vaughn opened shops in Williams, Arizona, and in California on Hollywood Boulevard situated across from Grauman's Chinese Theater. In Williams, Vaughn employed Randall Honwesima (Hopi) and hired Homer Vance (Hopi) to work in Hollywood. Reese Vaughn retired to Phoenix in 1948.

Vaughn created shop marks to be used by his silversmiths: one simply states VAUGHN'S, and the other includes VAUGHN'S with a stepped thunderbird figure.

1- Four butterfly pins, all marked. Top two have star hallmark for John Silver (Navajo); bottom left has shop mark for Gallup Mercantile or its subsidiary Gallup Indian Jewelry; bottom right has shop mark for Vaughn's Indian Store.

2- Charming cow head pin with dangling bell, marked with VAUGHN'S STERLING shop mark, mid-1930s.

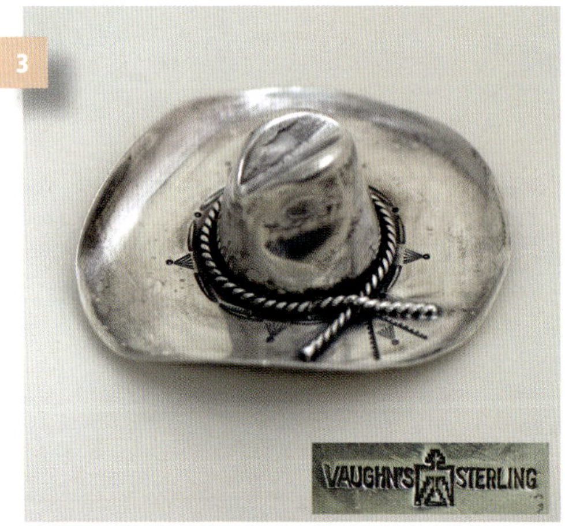

3- Silver cowboy hat ashtray, c. 1935, marked VAUGHN'S STERLING. This piece is nearly identical to cowboy hat ashtrays made at Southwest Arts and Crafts in Santa Fe.

4- Hopi silversmith Randall Honwesima, late 1930s. Postcard image was taken at Vaughn's in Williams, Arizona, where he worked from 1937 until 1962. He learned from Hopi silversmith Grant Jenkins in the early 1930s.

Fred Wilson's Indian Trading Post

In 1936, Fred Wilson acquired Vaughn's Indian Store in Phoenix and operated it as Fred Wilson's Indian Trading Post. Through the years, he opened and closed many branches from Salt Lake City to Lake Arrowhead, California, to Coolidge, New Mexico, as well as in hotels in the Phoenix area. He employed many Indian silversmiths until the 1950s, including Morris Robinson (Hopi), Ralph Tawangyawma (Hopi), and Sam Roanhorse (Navajo).

Wilson was an advocate of the Indian Arts and Crafts Board's silver stamping program, and was an early member of the UITA. He retired from the retail Indian art business in 1962. About 1940 Fred Wilson created a shop mark from his business logo using the initials of his name with the "F" over the "W" connecting in the center.

2- Fred Wilson's Indian Trading Post advertisement in a 1938 national magazine promoting a Hopi silver salad set. The "Master Silversmith" mentioned in the ad was Morris Robinson.

1- Fred Wilson bought Vaughn's Indian Store at 25-27 North Central Avenue, Phoenix, in 1936. Not only was it "Arizona's largest curio store," but it also employed many Hopi and Navajo silversmiths.

3- Three dragonfly pins. The two with turquoise settings are unmarked, possibly Navajo, Pueblo, or Hopi made. Bottom right pin is marked with the shop mark for Fred Wilson's Indian Trading Post in Phoenix and made by Morris Robinson (Hopi).

4- Spiderweb turquoise pin marked with the FW shop mark used by silversmiths who worked at Fred Wilson's Indian Trading Post, Phoenix.

Thunderbird Shop

On May 26, 1909, Angela Patania and her children boarded the *S.S. San Giorgio* sailing from Palermo, Italy, to reunite in New York with Giovanni, her husband who had immigrated a few years earlier. The oldest son, Francesco, or Frank as he would be known in America, was born in Sicily in 1899. As a boy he apprenticed to a goldsmith in Italy for four years, and, about 1918, he would find work as a designer with Goldsmith & Stern, a prominent jewelry firm in New York City. In 1923, Patania developed tuberculosis and was sent by his employer to Santa Fe for treatment. During his two years of convalescence, he continued to draw designs and sent them back to New York.

Bracelet, earrings, and ring made by Frank Patania Sr. *Courtesy White collection.*

Patania was immediately enamored by the Southwest and realized he did not wish to return to New York. Upon encountering southwestern Indian jewelry, he found the direction his career would ultimately follow. Patania opened his own business in 1927 on the plaza in Santa Fe, originally naming it Thunderbird Curios. The name changed shortly afterward to Thunderbird Shop. Frank's younger brother Carmelo, nicknamed Pat, joined him in Santa Fe where he would manage the shop and apprentice as a silversmith. In 1930, Frank married Aurora Masocco, and they would have three children together. Frank Jr. was born in 1932. Aurora assisted in managing the business, designing the look of the shop, and maintaining a welcoming atmosphere.

Advertising sticker with image of shop mark used by the Thunderbird Shop.

By this time, Patania was gaining recognition for his designs and exquisite craftsmanship, for displaying attention to detail, and for using only the highest-quality settings of turquoise and coral. As the business grew, he required help in the shop and hired Native American silversmiths to work under his supervision. The first may likely have been Charles Begay, a Navajo who was employed in 1934. The next year Lewis Lomay, a Hopi who had been hired to paint pictures in the shop, would instead take up silversmithing tools and put away his brushes. Thus began the Thunderbird Shop's long association with American Indian and Hispanic silversmiths, who would be employed as bench smiths for many decades.

Looking to expand, Patania opened a second shop in downtown Tucson in 1937. Afterward, the family would spend summers in Santa Fe and winters in Tucson, and many of their silversmiths would do the same. Miranda Masocco, Aurora's sister, worked as a designer and managed the shop in Santa Fe while Carmelo managed the shop in Tucson during Frank and Aurora's seasonal absences.

After World War II and into the 1950s, the Thunderbird Shop continued to garner national and international recognition. Modern-design crafts and jewelry were in vogue, and Patania's designs were more popular than ever. Commissions were common, and many monogrammed and special order items were made in both shops.

Frank Patania Jr. spent his childhood in the Santa Fe and Tucson shops, not only amusing the customers but apprenticing under his father to become a silversmith. In 1954, he married, fathering three children, and the third generation of Patania silversmiths, Samuel, was born in 1961. Frank Jr. had joined the Thunderbird Shop in 1956 as a full-time employee at the Tucson location. By 1962, he was acquiring national attention for the simplicity and elegance of his designs.

With the passing of Frank Sr. in 1964, and the family now firmly rooted in Tucson, Aurora closed the Santa Fe shop when the lease expired that same year. Frank Jr. continued to work in the Tucson shop, and the craftsmen worked under his direction. Frank Jr. would reopen the Santa Fe Thunderbird Shop in 1968 in a new location just off the plaza, but no silversmiths were ever employed in that location. Though Frank Jr. is still an active jeweler, he closed the Santa Fe Thunderbird Shop in 2007.

1- Turquoise necklace attributed to Frank Patania Sr. by his son Frank Jr. Coral necklace designed by Frank Sr. but made by another silversmith in the Thunderbird Shop. Both pieces signed with oval FP mark. *Courtesy Karen Sires.*

2- Thunderbird Shop commissioned items: thunderbird pin; earrings for Santa Fe Fiesta Council; Tohono pin for Tucson Festival Society, 1950s; bolo for Tucson Sunshine Climate Club, 1950s–1960s. Multiple quantity items were designed by hand, cast by an eastern company, and then hand-finished in the shop.

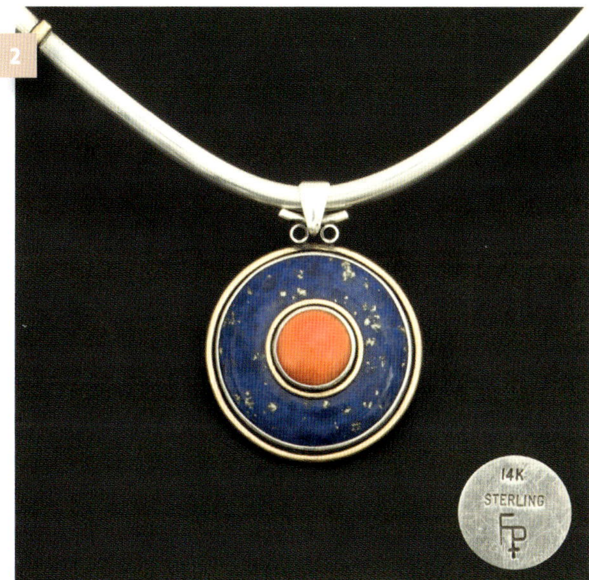

1- Plain silver bracelet and turquoise bracelet made by silversmiths in the Thunderbird Shop using Patania designs.

2- Pendant or enhancer of lapis, coral, sterling silver, and 14-karat gold made by Frank Patania Jr. *Courtesy Michael Schultz.*

3- Tufa-cast and jasper belt buckle by Frank Patania Jr.

Charm bracelet made by Sam Patania.

Sam started taking classes from his father in 1976 and became a full-time apprentice at the Tucson shop in 1979. He took jewelry classes in high school and at the University of Arizona to further his technical and design skills. In 1990, Sam took over operations at the Tucson shop, and longtime Thunderbird silversmith Dan Enos (Akimel O'odham, formerly Pima) continued to work with him. Sam renamed the shop Patania's Sterling Silver Originals and moved to a new location in 1994. Sometime later he closed the shop and now works out of his own studio. Sam's son, Marco, started working beside his father in 2012 to become the fourth-generation Patania to carry on the traditions of beautiful handcrafted jewelry.

Frank Patania Jr. and Sam Patania in 2008 at Bahti Indian Arts. *Courtesy Cathy Morrison.*

Confirming the importance of the contributions that the Patania family has made to American jewelry design, the Renwick Gallery, a branch of the Smithsonian American Art Museum, in 2000 acquired three bracelets, one each from Frank Sr., Frank Jr., and Sam, for their permanent collection.

Silver bracelet with stamp and chisel design on front and appliqué quail on the inside by Carmelo "Pat" Patania. *Private collection.*

For over twenty years, until his retirement in 1980, another member of the Patania family contributed to the legacy set forth by his brother. Carmelo Patania opened the Kachina Shop in Tucson in 1959 and made distinctive silver jewelry of his own designs. He based his creations on the designs of his brother and often added a bold and whimsical touch. Carmelo passed away in 1999; he marked his work with a block CP.

In 2009, Frank Patania Jr. published an explanation of the Thunderbird Shop hallmarks on his website. The following information is culled from Frank Jr.'s research and personal interviews the authors conducted with him and Sam.

Frank Patania Sr. did not hallmark most of his earliest creations; however, his most important pieces were marked with a rocker-engraved FP made in a diamond shape. After a time, Patania decided the work being made in the shop should be marked in some way. A thunderbird hallmark was designed, and the Patania family believes this mark was first used in the late 1930s in conjunction with a sterling stamp. Only two Thunderbird Shop stamps were made, one for the Tucson location and one for Santa Fe. According to Frank Jr., placement of the FP and thunderbird stamps around the "sterling" mark can distinguish which silversmith made the piece. Less complex and repetitive shop designs, including spoon sets, were made by the bench smiths, with all work organized and supervised by Patania family members. Some of these items were marked only with the thunderbird and "sterling" stamps. Bench smiths were not allowed to use their personal hallmark, if they had one, on shop work. Frank Jr. said, "I had thought of having dies made for the marks of our most skilled smiths, such as Jimmie Herald and Dan Enos, to use along with the FP and thunderbird. I regret that I never got around to doing it; they deserved to be recognized for their exceptional craftsmanship."

In the early to mid-1940s, Frank Sr. designed a personal hallmark of a conjoined offset FP which, with the thunderbird shop and "sterling" marks, were stamped on pieces Frank Sr. made as well as on pieces he designed that were made by the silversmiths under his supervision.

In the 1950s, new dies were made with the same conjoined offset FP but set inside an oval. This die was typically used to distinguish more important pieces made by Frank Sr. or pieces made under his supervision. At the same time, another die was made of a stylized script FP enclosed in a thin oval line; this mark was used by Frank Sr. on outstanding work that he created.

Pieces handmade by Frank Patania Sr. exhibit complicated and elegant work, obviously made by a master craftsman. He would not have concerned himself with mundane pieces that the bench smiths could easily have made. But while he was creating his masterworks, he would have had bench smiths make the bezels, drops, and other simple parts that he would then assemble into his work of art.

In 1956, when Frank Jr. began working full-time, he used the Thunderbird Shop system of hallmarking for bench smiths, stamping FP, the thunderbird mark, and sterling. After 1964, he designed his own hallmark, using the conjoined offset FP but adding by hand a horizontal line across the bottom of the "P," and, in 1980, he had this mark made into a die.

When Sam took charge of the Tucson shop in the late 1980s, the standard hallmarking system continued. In 1985, Sam devised his own hallmark, an "S" with a vertical line passing through the lower part to form a "P." By 1990, Sam decided to make his stamp a continuation of his father's and grandfather's to represent all three generations in one hallmark; he started with the offset conjoined FP, added the horizontal line to the bottom of the "P" that his dad used, and then added an "S" underneath the "P." In 2001, he started using a ".925" stamp because it was smaller than a "sterling" stamp.

Many American Indian artists were employed in the Thunderbird Shop, some as painters but most as silversmiths. In the Santa Fe shop, as many as five or six smiths worked at one time; and in the smaller Tucson workshop, up to four smiths. They worked on special orders and everyday pieces. Frank Sr. would sketch out the design, select the stones to be used, and supervise the construction of the pieces they worked on.

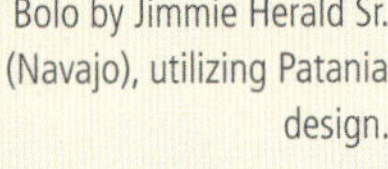
Bolo by Jimmie Herald Sr. (Navajo), utilizing Patania design.

The Patania family developed an exceptional relationship with Native American silversmiths in both shops. At least sixty silversmiths—Indian, Hispanic, and Anglo—apprenticed and worked for them over the decades, and many remained loyal to the Patanias, continuing in their employ until retirement. Hopi Lewis Lomay hired on in 1934 and stayed for eight years. In 1938, Frank Sr. hired a Navajo by the name of Jimmie Herald, who would work in the Santa Fe and Tucson shops until his retirement in the mid-1970s. His brother, Herbert Herald, worked in Tucson in the late 1940s and through the 1950s; and his son, Jimmie Herald Jr., also worked in the Tucson shop for some time. Jimmie's brother-in-law, Daniel Enos, hired on in the early 1950s and remained a valued employee until his retirement in 1992. Two other silversmiths of note who worked at the Thunderbird Shop were Harry Sakyesva (Hopi) and Julian Lovato from Kewa (Santo Domingo) Pueblo.

A poignant example of Frank Sr.'s relationship with his Indian employees is evidenced by Waldo Mootzka, a Hopi from Oraibi. Mootzka was employed by Patania in 1934, or possibly sooner. He started by painting pictures of Hopi kachinas to be sold in the shop; then Patania taught him silversmithing. Mootzka was killed in a car accident between Tucson and Phoenix, and when Patania heard of his death he sent a heartfelt letter, dated June 30, 1938, to Indian art patron Leslie Van Ness Denman of San Francisco informing her of the news. In it he stated, "He has been with us for so many years, that we felt his passing away very deeply."

Hopicrafts

Emory and Wayne Sekaquaptewa, brothers from the Hopi village of Hotevilla, learned to make silver from an experienced smith, Harry Sakyesva (Hopi), before 1960 while they were all residing in Phoenix. They soon opened a business called Hopi Enterprises, which contracted to make jewelry commissioned by area businesses and organizations including the Phoenix City Council and the National Park Service. Sakyesva continued to work for the new business, and three other Hopis—Bernard Dawahoya, Eldon James, and Glenn Lucas—were hired. In 1962, the shop relocated to Kykotsmovi and was renamed Hopicrafts.

The Sekaquaptewas created a piecework system where several smiths would perform individual operations in the creation of one piece. According to Emory Sekaquaptewa, piecework was mainly used for training purposes, and those pieces would be marked only with the Hopicrafts shop mark of a conjoined capital "H" and lowercase "C." Silversmiths whose work was in high demand, such as Bernard Dawahoya and Glenn Lucas, would use their individual hallmark along with the shop mark.

1- Pin, pill box, and earrings made by bench smiths at Hopicrafts.

2- Jewelry made by Hopi silversmiths working at Hopicrafts. Bolo by Steven Sockyma, ring by Virgil Thomas, Hohokam-design pin by Elgene Sehongva, bracelet by Mitchell Sockyma.

All Hopicrafts jewelry was made in the overlay style with very few turquoise settings and featured a textured pattern in the background of the cutout area. A satin finish was used to enhance the beauty of their own highly distinctive designs. Close attention was paid to detail, even to the handmade silver tips for the ends of bolo ties.

According to Emory, the hallmark SEKAQUAPTEWA was used by his brother Wayne and himself, though Wayne was mostly involved in business matters and never made much silver. Wayne passed away in 1979, and Hopicrafts closed in 1983; Emory continued to make silver until his death in 2007.

1- Overlay bracelet made by Emory Sekaquaptewa (Hopi).

2- Bracelet by Phillip Sekaquaptewa (Hopi), made while working at Hopicrafts using his first hallmark. *Courtesy White collection.*

3- Appliqué and inlaid bracelet and overlay Crow Mother Kachina pendant made by Phillip Sekaquaptewa (Hopi), marked with a later hallmark incorporating his Hopi name. *Private collection.*

Among the artists who trained and worked at Hopicrafts was Phillip Sekaquaptewa, the son of co-founder Wayne Sekaquaptewa. Phil began his career in the early 1970s, and his work was grounded in the overlay tradition, but he was an early innovator of expanding design capabilities including tufa casting and multistone inlays. His later designs used gold and precious stones. He won many awards from prestigious Indian art shows, and, if his life had not been cut short in 2003, he surely would have had a long and distinguished career. His hallmarks include a bird track with either the Hopicrafts shop mark or his initials PS; the last mark he used was "Weseoma" in cursive with a tadpole below.

White Hogan

John Bonnell came to Arizona in 1936, and in 1939 he was managing Fred Wilson's Indian Trading Post in Phoenix. Before 1946, John and his wife, Virginia, moved to Flagstaff to open their own Indian craft business. They partnered with two Navajo silversmiths, cousins Kenneth Begay and Allen Kee, to establish the White Hogan Silver Shop, which advertised itself as "Home of the World's Most Distinctive Indian Silver." The business relocated a few times before settling into downtown Scottsdale in 1951.

Advertising sticker used by the White Hogan, Scottsdale.

Begay's and Kee's designs were simple, elegant, and modern, with minimal decoration and general lack of turquoise settings. It diverged greatly from traditional Indian jewelry. According to Bonnell, the only tools used in the shop were cold chisel, hammer, saw, and file.

Salt dip (2.5" wide), handmade by Kenneth Begay (Navajo); salt spoon cast from White Hogan design.

One of the first major competitions White Hogan entered was rocked by controversy when White Hogan won an unprecedented sixty-six ribbons in the silver division at the Gallup Inter-Tribal Ceremonial in 1950. The awards included First Grand Prize in Navajo Silver, the Elkus Award for "new silver objects that will have commercial value and open a new field for Indian silver handcrafts," and an award for winning the largest number of awards. Established Gallup traders fumed at the upset and, in an article in the *Gallup Independent*, dismissed White Hogan as "an upstart, a self-promoter, a minnow in the sea of Indian silversmith history."

In the same article, Bonnell answered the critics by explaining that White Hogan was attempting to combat the "sweatshop mentality in the Indian jewelry field," where most silversmiths were sorely underpaid. "We treat our workers like human beings. Every three months we divide net profits with the Indians working for us. We also pay them higher base salaries than any trader in the Gallup area," Bonnell explained. He also attributed the White Hogan's success completely to the talents of Kenneth Begay and Allen Kee.

1- Silver jewelry inlaid with ironwood made at the White Hogan. Bolo tie (left) by Allen Kee (Navajo); buckle and bolo (right) by George Kee (Navajo). *Courtesy White collection.*

2- Lidded containers made of ironwood and silver by Navajo silversmiths associated with the White Hogan. Hinged box (left) by George Kee; ironwood bowl (front center) with silver lid and Pilot Mountain turquoise knob made around 2000 by Edison Cummings; square box and box (right) both by John Begay.

3- Two square nut dishes made by Sam Roanhorse (Navajo) while working at the White Hogan

The White Hogan continued its dominance in competitions throughout the 1950s. Begay began incorporating Arizona ironwood into his designs by 1952, and in May of that year the White Hogan had accumulated an astonishing 558 ribbons, including many grand prizes, in nine exhibits in the Southwest. At the 1956 Gallup Ceremonial, the White Hogan set a record for winning 98 ribbons, the most ever won in a single division.

Business increased so that, by 1956, three other Navajo silversmiths were working alongside Kenneth Begay and Allen Kee. The profit-sharing plan enacted at the outset of the business was still intact as late as 1963, and it was the only one of its kind involving Indian artists.

Many Navajo silversmiths learned and worked at the White Hogan through the years, several with familial connections to the founding smiths. Allen Kee's brothers Ivan and George were employed there, and Kenneth Begay's brother Johnnie Mike and son Harvey also worked for the Bonnells. Kenneth Begay's designs influenced generations of Indian silversmiths, whether through direct or indirect contact, and changed the style of contemporary Native jewelry. The White Hogan became one of the most influential Indian silver shops and continued winning prizes at arts and crafts exhibits throughout the Southwest. The shop distinguished itself not only by its modern jewelry designs, but also by its exquisite flatware and hollowware for table settings and vessels of ironwood with silver decoration.

Silver bracelet inlaid with ironwood by Kenneth Begay (Navajo) and earrings by Allen Kee (Navajo). *Courtesy Karen Sires.*

Jon Bonnell and his wife, Paulla, took over the shop after his father's death in 1973, and shortly afterward George Kee left to work for Arizona Turquoise and Silver Company in Scottsdale. When Jon Bonnell decided to close White Hogan in August 2006, two silversmiths, John Begay and Jonathan Mike, were the last of the Navajo artists to work for this significant silver shop. John Begay told the *Arizona Republic* that he had worked there for more than two decades.

Nut dishes handmade by Michael Carroll (Navajo), spiral ring by Leroy Turquoise (Navajo). Remaining items cast from Kenneth Begay designs; the hallmarks include Kenneth Begay's and the shop mark for White Hogan. A great quantity of the salt spoons were cast beginning as early as 1952.

Nearly all silver made at the White Hogan was stamped with a trademark of a Navajo hogan. This mark was originally designed and used by Fred Peshlakai and sold to the White Hogan through Kenneth Begay, who was Peshlakai's student at Fort Wingate Indian School. In 1983, Jon Bonnell filed for a patent of the shop mark stating the mark was first used in 1948. Most of the silversmiths also incorporated an individual hallmark of their initials along with the hogan shop mark. Some pieces were stamped HAND MADE whereas others were etched with "hand made" and "original design." White Hogan made a practice of replicating certain Kenneth Begay designs by casting methods, especially the signature spiral design in earrings, cuff links, and pendants as well as salt spoons and some simple bracelets. Only items stamped or etched with HAND MADE are unquestionably hand fabricated by the artist.

Chapter 5:

The Government and the Guilds

Indian Arts and Crafts Board

The Indian Arts and Crafts Board (IACB), an agency of the Department of the Interior, was formally established in 1936 to aid in the revitalization and promotion of traditional Native American arts. The preservation of traditional southwest Indian silverwork was one of the most urgent issues to be addressed by the board.

1- Bracelets (1938–1943), all marked U.S.NAVAJO by the Indian Arts and Crafts Board. The designating numbers were 4 for Fred Harvey Company (top); 40 for Fort Wingate Indian School (far left and bottom right); and 2 for C. G. Wallace (second from left front and far right).

2- Two silver pins, both stamped with Indian Arts and Crafts Board mark U.S.NAVAJO 60, indicating they were made at the Santa Fe Indian School, 1938–1943.

Competition from manufacturers of Indian-design jewelry, such as Maisel's, was making it nearly impossible for individual Indian silversmiths to make a living. A series of meetings held by the board resulted in a program by which genuine handmade Navajo, Pueblo, and Hopi silver could obtain a stamp of authenticity from the government. An announcement, made in March 1937, set forth the standards by which jewelry could qualify for the stamp, and that the stamp "should be applied only to the finest quality of wholly genuine, truly hand-fashioned and authentic Indian silver and turquoise products."

The IACB silver stamping program has been examined at length by Jonathan Batkin in his excellent book *The Native American Curio Trade in New Mexico*. Batkin explains how this program adopted hallmarks that were stamped on silver individually produced and entirely handmade (no power-driven machinery could be used) from silver slugs hammered to shape; the turquoise also had to be genuine, untreated, and cut and polished by hand.

Four bracelets with Indian Arts and Crafts Board marks, 1938–1943. Top cast bracelet with mark U.S.ZUNI 1 assigned to C. G. Wallace; bottom left marked U.S.NAVAJO 5 for Kelsey Trading or Pueblo Indian Arts and Crafts; middle and far right U.S.NAVAJO 1 for Gallup Mercantile.

Only an agent of the IACB could determine which silver complied with the standards and therefore could receive the government mark. No jewelry with tourist-type designs, such as arrow stamps, were eligible to receive the hallmark. C. G. Wallace had a bracelet with such stamps rejected. But silver made by casting in an individual tufa mold was approved to receive the government stamp, as evidenced by a cast bracelet by Juan De Dios marked with U.S.ZUNI 1.

Kenneth Chapman, curator of the Laboratory of Anthropology in Santa Fe, and a respected authority on southwest Indian arts, assumed responsibility as special agent for the silver program. It was Chapman who developed the marking system for approved silver, spending months in research until he and Ambrose Roanhorse, a well-respected Navajo silversmith who taught at the Santa Fe Indian School, settled on the small dies that were eventually put into service.

The marks included the letters "U.S." and then the tribal identification, NAVAJO, ZUNI, HOPI, and RGPUEBLO (for Rio Grande Pueblo) followed by a number identifying the participating trader, wholesaler, or federal Indian school. Stamps were designed and made for HOPI and RGPUEBLO, but apparently never used, possibly because there were no interested traders who employed Pueblo or Hopi smiths.

Ambrose Roanhorse was responsible for applying the stamp to approved pieces, and later Dooley Shorty, the silversmithing teacher at Fort Wingate Indian School, also did some marking of approved silver.

The first numbers were assigned and stamped under Chapman's supervision on April 5, 1938, in Santa Fe. Chapman and Roanhorse then traveled throughout New Mexico to stamp the silver held in anticipation of the start of the program. After three weeks, Chapman estimated that 4,000 pieces were examined in the first batches of silver with 2,322 qualifying for the stamp.

Response to the program was mixed. C. G. Wallace was enthusiastic and sent many pieces of silver for marking during the life of the program. On the other hand, Herman Schweizer was cautious about the objectives of the program, but still submitted some of the first articles stamped in April 1938, thinking the Harvey Company should be in on the ground floor.

These two silver pins were stamped by the Indian Arts and Crafts Board with U.S.NAVAJO 2, indicating they were made for C. G. Wallace, 1938–1943. Bottom pin also includes unknown artist's hallmark of curved arrow.

Complaints arose quickly. Traders and silversmiths were concerned that the rules were too stringent. Even C. G. Wallace, the program's biggest supporter, complained to Chapman that he had to put a man on the road to try to sell the stamped silver because his biggest clients, the Fred Harvey Company and the Gallup wholesale houses, had turned their backs on Wallace's government-stamped jewelry.

Schweizer's support of the program was short lived, and he quickly concluded it was a failure. He told Chapman the IACB had not advertised the program as promised, and the traveling public knew nothing about it. When tourists were shown the marked silver they became suspicious of the unmarked silver in the store. Schweizer ceased selling government-stamped silver by late 1938.

Despite the lack of success of the silver stamping program, the IACB made additional efforts to help individual Indian groups form cooperatives and guilds to better market their own handicrafts. For example, in 1940 the Pueblo Indian Arts and Crafts Market, a cooperative of Pueblo Indian artists, was organized in Albuquerque. The aim of these cooperatives was to improve and to increase the production and the sale of all handicrafts of individual tribes.

Silver submitted to Chapman for stamping gradually slowed, and the program waned even more with the outbreak of World War II. The last record in Chapman's notes of items submitted were from the Santa Fe Indian School, which sent only three pieces for marking in June 1943.

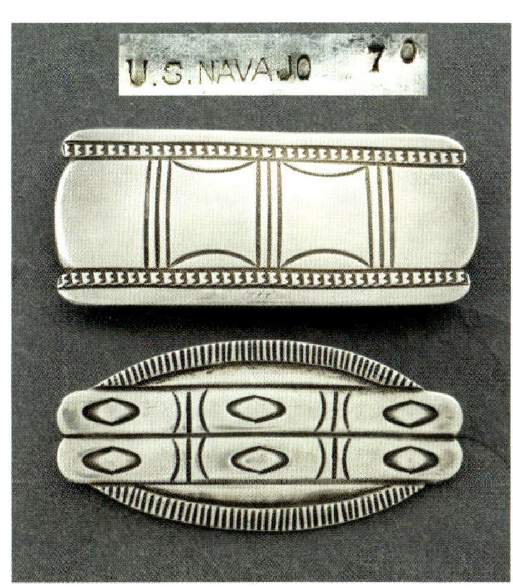

Two silver pins stamped with Indian Arts and Crafts Board mark U.S.NAVAJO 70, designating they were made for the Navajo Arts and Crafts Guild, 1940–1943. This number was originally assigned by Chapman in March 1940.

NO.	TRADER OR SCHOOL	LOCATION
U.S. NAVAJO		
1	Gallup Mercantile Company	Gallup, NM
2	C. G. Wallace	Zuni, NM
3	Berton I. Staples, Crafts del Navajo	Coolidge, NM
4	Fred Harvey Company	Albuquerque, NM
5	Kelsey Trading Company*	Zuni, NM
	Pueblo Indian Arts and Craft Market*	Albuquerque, NM
6	Zuni Trading Post (Robert Wallace)	Zuni, NM
10	Tuba City Indian School	Tuba City, AZ
11	Drolet's Trading Post (J. M. Drolet)	Naschitti, NM
20	Shiprock Indian School	Shiprock, AZ
30	Crownpoint Indian School	Crownpoint, NM
40	Fort Wingate Indian School	Fort Wingate, NM
50	Albuquerque Indian School	Albuquerque, NM
60	Santa Fe Indian School	Santa Fe, NM
70	Navajo Arts and Crafts Guild	Fort Wingate, NM
U.S. ZUNI		
1	C. G. Wallace	Zuni, NM
4	Fred Harvey Company	Albuquerque, NM
5	Kelsey Trading Company*	Zuni, NM
	Pueblo Indian Arts and Craft Market*	Albuquerque, NM
6	Zuni Trading Post (Robert Wallace)	Zuni, NM
11	Gallup Mercantile Company	Gallup, NM

* It appears the numbers U.S.NAVAJO 5 and U.S.ZUNI 5 were reassigned in 1941. Kelsey Trading Company in Zuni was originally assigned those numbers and had 170 pieces stamped in April 1938. Kelsey must have stepped away from the program because Chapman notes on June 10, 1941, that he marked 36 pieces U.S.ZUNI 5 and thirteen pieces U.S.NAVAJO 5 received from the Pueblo Indian Arts and Crafts Market.

1- Handmade copper tray, c. 1940, with Keresan Pueblo Koshare (clown) design (13" dia.). This and the nearly identical tray to its right have matching Koshare designs, yet are different in detail, and were made by two different artists.

2- On the back of this tray is stamped in ink, "Hand Wrought Copper by Pueblo Indians of New Mexico Reservation Made." Possibly made in association with the Pueblo Indian Arts and Crafts Market organized at Albuquerque with the aid of the Indian Arts and Crafts Board.

Navajo Arts and Crafts Guild

The foundation for a future Navajo arts and crafts guild was laid in 1939 when a craft program was established at Fort Wingate with assistance from the Bureau of Indian Affairs. Ambrose Roanhorse was selected as director of the project, the purpose of which was to provide employment for the craftsmen who had learned their trade at federal Indian schools as well as for established silversmiths in the vicinity. Roanhorse distributed supplies on the reservation and collected finished work to be sold through the guild. By 1940, the project was being called the Navajo Arts and Crafts Guild (NACG), though it was not formally chartered by the tribal council until 1941, at which time it moved to Window Rock.

Two cast Yei pins marked on the back PINE SPRINGS. This hallmark could possibly originate from the short-lived Navajo tribal cooperative at Pine Springs, c. 1942. *Courtesy Karen Sires.*

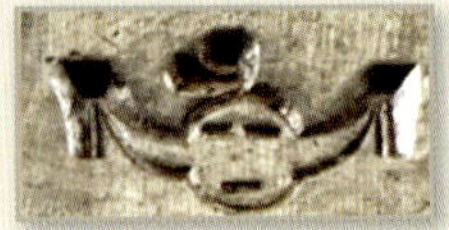

Bolo, buckle, and two pins made for the Navajo Arts and Crafts Guild, 1940s–1950s.

Craft items were produced either at the guild shop, in the homes of the craftsmen, or at community workshops already established on the reservation. Materials and supplies were issued only to craftsmen who could meet the standards and requirements for quality established by the guild. These standards were similar to those of the Indian Arts and Crafts Board program—though craftsmen having their own materials, supplies, and workshops could offer their products for sale to the guild. A full-time manager was hired, and one of the first was John Adair.

The UITA, in 1943, complained that the NACG was in direct competition with the traders. The controversy continued in 1946 during the Gallup Inter-Tribal Ceremonial when Arthur Woodward, one of the judges of the silversmithing division, was shocked to learn that the craftsmen who worked with the NACG were not permitted to submit their work for competition. The Ceremonial board contended that the Navajo Guild was government subsidized and should be disqualified; Woodward refuted their claim in an open letter published in the *Gallup Independent* newspaper, saying that guild craftsmen were in business for themselves and questioned whether the Gallup traders feared their silver would fare poorly in competition with the silver made by guild craftsmen.

Despite complaints from the reservation traders, the guild continued to succeed and to grow, and Ned Hatathli was named the first Navajo manager in 1951. In 1964, it opened its first branch at Cameron, Arizona, under the management of Kenneth Begay. By 1966, the NACG had added a branch at Betatakin (Navajo National Monument) with branches opening at Kayenta, Teec Nos Pos, and Chinle.

In 1971, the guild became the Navajo Arts and Crafts Enterprise (NACE), and under poor management, mistakes were made that nearly bankrupted the organization. Having lost a large sum of money, the enterprise survived only by scaling back its operations and closing many of its branches. Under new management, the NACE continues to be the only Navajo Nation-owned business engaged in the purchase and sale of Navajo-made arts and crafts.

Bracelet made for Navajo Arts and Crafts Guild, 1940s. *Courtesy White collection.*

The title Navajo Arts and Crafts Guild and its Horned Moon logo were registered with the U.S. Patent and Trademark Office in 1943. Items made through the NACG were marked with the Horned Moon logo and sometimes included the word NAVAJO. Rarely are individual silversmiths' hallmarks found on these pieces.

Museum of Northern Arizona Silver Project

The Museum of Northern Arizona (MNA) was founded in Flagstaff in 1928 by Harold and Mary-Russell Colton, who together defined its mission. One of their early undertakings was to revive Hopi arts and crafts that were suffering declines in the late 1920s, concentrating on pottery, basketry, and weaving. Silversmithing, on the other hand, was overlooked by the museum because it was a craft practiced on the reservation by a few men on a part-time basis. Paul Saufkie was the only skilled silversmith on the reservation in 1938; the isolation of the Hopi mesas had caused the others to leave for employment in curio shops around the Southwest.

Mary-Russell Colton began forming plans, as early as 1937, to make Hopi silver more distinctive and unique. Discussing her ideas in a letter to Kenneth Chapman, Colton thought Hopi silver was "practically without character, just more poor 'Navajo'" and that, "in very rare instances has it occurred to the Hopi smith to use Hopi design." Her conclusion was that "there is only one way to make Hopi silversmithing worth while, it must be *different* from any other Indian silversmithing." She hoped to encourage the Hopis to use designs unique to their own culture, applying them in a manner appearing "modern," and simplifying the jewelry, making it clean and elegant. "Thus," she wrote, "the Hopi could make a borrowed art their own."

Between November 1938 and March 1939, Colton sent letters to at least sixteen Hopi silversmiths, many addressed to the owners of the curios stores that employed them. Each letter contained her ideas for new Hopi designs and a copy of the Indian Arts and Crafts Board regulations explaining the advantage of receiving the government stamp. She also urged those contacted to place their personal hallmarks on the silver. Each smith that was interested in the project would receive an order from Colton with a photograph of a design from which to work, and she suggested the resulting jewelry should be made in accordance with the IACB standards. She hoped that in short time the smiths would be making their own Hopi designs and the museum designs would no longer be needed.

Some of the silversmiths who received letters were Randall Honwesima, Lewis Lomayesva, Harry Nasewytewa, Morris Robinson, Paul Saufkie, Ralph Tawangyawma, and Homer Vance. The letters sparked mixed reactions, both from the silversmiths and the curio store owners: some were enthusiastic, some ignored it completely, and still others were opposed to the idea. Three silversmiths working in Phoenix and Tucson even responded to Colton's letter personally. The following handwritten letter was signed by all three silversmiths:

We three Hopi Indian Silversmiths talked over the plans of yours, and have come to conclusion.

We are very sorry to say that we can not cooperate with you on your plan about the Government Stamps for our genuine Ind. Silver work.

White people & Mexicans copying Ind. Silver designs, then White people put the Snake Dance on at Prescott every year, and the Government says that he can not stop them. For these reasons we have thought things over very carefully.

What is the use depend on the Government now?

You said that we are using the Navajo Ind. Design on our silverwork, that is not so. We make stamps and dies using our own Hopi Ind. design, putting the decoration on our silverwork is also our own Hopi Ind. ideas. We are very sorry to that we are afraid that you do not know the Hopi design.

Now, as for the use of the Hopi Ind. design exclusively we are afraid this is going to be impossible for us to do, as you might know this, when the customer comes around to us to do the work for them, they usually have their own designs & ideas of the silverwork that they want, and if we expect to get a job, we have to copy the work, whether it is a Navajo, Zuni, or Hopi we have to do it.

You sent us the pottery design, that design is all right for pottery work. But we are not making pottery.

We are sending the picture back to you as we are not interested in making anything for you. We rather use our own designs, not Govt. stamp.

By the way how much was you going to charge us for Government stamps?

We hope you understand. White people always stealing the Ind. design, but the Govt. has no laws to stop that.

Yours very sincerely
Harry A. Nasewytewa
Morris Robinson
Ralph Tawangyawma

Fred Wilson enclosed the foregoing letter, which he confirmed was "entirely of their own conclusions," with a letter of his own addressed to Mrs. Colton, dated March 28, 1939. He advised that Morris and Ralph worked for him and that Harry was employed by Petty's of Tucson. He also criticized the IACB program because "Morris and Ralph are producing their own original designs, jewelry and silverwork of great beauty and public acceptance and I cannot grant the Board the unconstitutional privilege of outlawing their efforts." He also explained to Mrs. Colton that he felt her project was a worthy one, and he advised his smiths to give it whatever support they felt they could.

Out of the smiths contacted, seven attempted to make jewelry for the Hopi Silver Project. Paul Saufkie was the most successful, and Randall Honwesima, employed at Vaughn's in Williams, was the only smith working in a curio shop to participate.

The project continued to grow under the support of Paul Saufkie, and at the 1941 Hopi Craftsman Exhibition, the new silver was a hit with the public. But after the 1942 exhibition, the shows were suspended until 1947 because of the war. The war basically led to the demise of Mary-Russell Colton's Hopi Silver Project. But her endeavors would play a large role in the future of Hopi silversmiths.

Items by Hopi students in the first veterans' silversmithing class, 1947–1949. Bracelet (left) by Valjean Joshevema Sr. Sunface pin by Orville Talayumptewa. Box by Starlie Lomayaktewa pictured in July 1950 *Arizona Highways*. Overlay bracelet (right) by Arthur Yowytewa and instructor Paul Saufkie.

Hopi Silvercraft Cooperative Guild

At the end of World War II, the Coltons, who were encouraged by Paul Saufkie's success with the designs suggested by the museum, urged respected Hopi artist Fred Kabotie to work on more distinctive silver designs that could be used by Hopi silversmiths. But little was accomplished until August 1946 when Kabotie invited Saufkie, his wife's brother, to display pieces of his jewelry at a Hopi arts and crafts sale at Shungopavi during the Snake Dance. Dr. Willard Beatty, Director of the Education Division of the Indian Services, attended the Snake Dance and was impressed with Saufkie's silver. He met with Kabotie and Saufkie the next day and discussed the need for returning Hopi war veterans to find jobs. Beatty proposed creating a school to teach silversmithing to the veterans utilizing funding provided by the G.I. Bill of Rights.

Fred Kabotie moved forward organizing the silver classes. Paul Saufkie was hired as technical director, teaching the students the methods of working silver and copper, and Kabotie was design instructor. The Veteran's Administration paid Saufkie's salary, purchased tools and materials, and paid each student a living allowance of about $65 a month. The classes were limited to fifteen students (although only thirteen enrolled in the first class) and were to last for eighteen months, commencing February 1947 at the Hopi High School in Oraibi.

Students practiced on copper until they were proficient to work in silver, which they learned the old way by casting ingots and hammering them into shape; no sheet silver was used. Likely some of the first tasks for students was to learn to make their own stamping dies, their individual hallmarks, and the Sunface symbol of the Hopi trademark.

Three pins, all cast silver, late 1940s, from Hopi veterans' classes. Lower left by Valjean Joshevema Sr.; middle unmarked, adapted from design by Museum of Northern Arizona; right by Tom Humiyestewa. *Courtesy Karen Sires.*

Jewelry designs for the G.I. Bill classes were drawn from many sources including traditional Hopi pottery, weaving, and textiles. Also incorporated were the Museum of Northern Arizona Silver Project designs and Mimbres figures from Kabotie's book *Designs from the Ancient Mimbreños: With a Hopi Interpretation*.

After students graduated from the first class in January 1949, they had few places to sell their wares and little capital to buy materials, so many ceased to make silver. Kabotie met with representatives from the Indian Arts and Crafts Board and the Hopi Agency to discuss the need for a steady market to enable the graduates to make and sell jewelry. The participants advanced the idea of forming a cooperative guild to benefit the silversmiths. Kabotie, Saufkie, and six of the graduating veterans set up a constitution and bylaws to form the Hopi Silvercraft Cooperative Guild in 1949. The Sunface trademark used by all students became the shop mark representing the guild. With a loan from the Bureau of Indian Affairs, the guild purchased silver, turquoise, and other necessary materials from wholesalers, and the silversmiths would reimburse the Hopi Guild after their items had been sold. The guild also functioned as a workshop for those members who lacked the tools or electricity to work at home.

Early Hopi veterans' classes jewelry, unsigned. Copper practice bracelet, cast silver ring with turquoise, and cast silver clip earrings, all late 1940s. Leather belt made by Herbert Komayouse (Quimayousie) signed with his name, hallmark, and Hopi trademark.

In July 1949, Fred Kabotie and Paul Saufkie took a large stock of finished jewelry from guild members to the Hopi Craftsman Exhibition at MNA for the first display and sale of their new designs; nearly every piece they took was sold.

Arizona Highways magazine in July 1950 published a color article by writer and photographer J. H. McGibbeny about the Hopi Guild and the new design jewelry; the article caused a great demand not only nationally, but worldwide. Kabotie was impelled to put together a mimeographed catalog later that year detailing prices and items available for wholesale and retail purchase. In the catalog, Kabotie specified five classifications of general types of jewelry made by the guild: overlay, cutout, cast, stamped, and copper inlay. Leather belts made by the silversmiths with Hopi designs accompanied silver buckles.

Pieces by students from the second Hopi veterans' class. Left bracelet by Tom Humiyestewa, center bracelet by Richard Kagenvema, bottom pin by Calvin Hastings, right pin by Walter Polelonema. No pieces have textured backgrounds.

Bracelet, earrings, and pins made by Douglas Holmes (Hopi, 1925–2005). From Moenkopi, he learned silversmithing in the second veterans' class and worked until 1961. He favored designs taken from Fred Kabotie's book *Designs from the Ancient Mimbreños: With a Hopi Interpretation*.

The second and final class of veterans graduated in January 1951. The work made in the veterans' classes shows varied techniques, including tufa-cast, overlay, and appliqué, with designs cut out or applied with repoussé and stamps. Turquoise was often used in settings or inlaid alone or with jet. Many of the techniques fell into disuse as the overlay technique became dominant, perhaps because of the simple clean lines that were becoming popular with the modernist movement. By the mid-1950s, overlay was the only technique used by guild silversmiths, turquoise settings had nearly disappeared, and the use of sheet silver replaced hand-hammered ingots.

Jewelry made by Wallie Sekayumptewa (Hopi, 1916–2003), from Hotevilla, who attended the second veterans' class. His largest production of silver was before 1967. He occasionally included turquoise settings with overlay and rarely textured the background of his pieces.

In 1963, the Hopi Guild moved from Oraibi to a newly constructed building on Second Mesa that included a large showroom and workshop space for the artists. Fred Kabotie worked with the guild in various ways, serving as president from 1960 until his retirement in 1971, and his son, Michael Kabotie, succeeded him as president for a few terms.

1- Overlay necklace, late 1950s, by Leroy Kewanyama (Hopi). *Courtesy Karen Sires.*

The Hopi Guild eventually allowed other craftspeople to join: potters, carvers, painters, textile and basket weavers. It also served as a source of marketing by setting up at fairs and trade shows. But the guild's main focus has always been on silver jewelry; that focus and the G.I. Bill classes after World War II changed the direction of Hopi silver into elegant modern designs that define it to the present day.

2- Jewelry by Hopi Silvercraft Guild silversmiths, c. 1960. Parrot earrings, Koyemsi (Mudhead) pin, and bracelet all by Ted Wadsworth (rabbit stick mark); buckle by McBride Lomayestewa (lightning mark); Koshare (clown) pin by Billie Ray Hawee (star and crescent moon mark). Only some of the pieces have textured backgrounds.

Over the years, the guild has had its ups and downs for many reasons—economic instability chiefly among them. At one time, the guild was the only place to sell finished jewelry for those working exclusively on the mesas. There were times that there were not enough silversmiths to create a quantity of jewelry to satisfy demand; the 1980s was an especially successful decade. Over time, other avenues of merchandising opened up, and many craftsmen were able to sell jewelry easier to other markets. As the Internet has become a valuable resource for buyers far from the Southwest, making it easier for craftsmen to sell directly to individuals, the guild has struggled to remain relevant.

Two pins and a buckle by Leroy Kewanyama (Hopi, 1922–1997). From Shungopavi, he learned silversmithing at the Guild in the mid-1950s and was also a noted painter. His jewelry often includes settings and was distinctive. Parrot pottery design pin is a rare example of Hopi chip inlay, c. 1970.

Chapter 6:

The Silversmiths

In 1893 the World's Columbian Exposition, commemorating the four hundredth anniversary of the voyage of Christopher Columbus, was held in Chicago. An Indian silversmith called Navajo Jake was at the exhibition, demonstrating his art of working silver into jewelry for an audience completely unfamiliar with his culture and way of life.

Between the 1890s and 1940s, jewelry emerged as one of the most profitable craft arts of the American Indian. Curio stores sprang up across the country and, to add an air of authenticity, Indian silversmiths were often hired to demonstrate and to sell their wares. The Fred Harvey Company employed a Navajo silversmith at the Alvarado Hotel in 1902, and as early as 1905 a Navajo silversmith was employed in a New York City curio shop.

In the 1920s, silversmithing shops like Southwest Arts and Crafts and Maisel's opened in New Mexico and provided an opportunity for silversmiths to work closer to home. More and more silversmiths—Navajo, Pueblo, and Hopi—found it easier to make a living by leaving the reservation to work seasonally, or even full-time, in curio stores from Los Angeles to Massachusetts and New York.

The silversmiths employed in urban areas were some of the first to use a personal hallmark on their work by the late 1920s or early 1930s, perhaps prompted by their employers. Eventually, silversmiths found value and recognition in signing their creations, and it became a custom for many well-known artists. Today, it is standard practice for silversmiths to use an identifying hallmark on their creations.

Ribbed bracelet, c. 1930. The "H" and coyote head marks were used by Grant Jenkins (Hopi); the mark on the right may possibly be for Pierce Kewanwytewa (Hopi). It is unknown why the two would have collaborated on this bracelet. *Private collection.*

GRANT JENKINS

(Hopi, c. 1903–1933)

Born at Moenkopi, Grant Jenkins relocated to Phoenix and, around 1924, he was working as a silversmith and also teaching his cousin Morris Robinson the basics of working silver. At the first Hopi Craftsman Exhibition held at the Museum of Northern Arizona in 1930, several pieces of work by Jenkins were displayed, including a "jewel box." During his short career, Jenkins was employed at a variety of stores in Phoenix, including Vaughn's Indian Store. While employed at Skiles Indian Shop, he taught silversmithing skills to a co-worker, Randall Honwesima (Hopi). Jenkins passed away in Phoenix on November 24, 1933. It is not known when he began to sign his work, as few examples are available for research, but his hallmark was a right-facing coyote head and a capital "H" for Hopi.

Four bracelets, c. 1930, made by Hopi silversmiths. Bracelet with two turquoise stones made by Grant Jenkins, single turquoise stone bracelet made by Homer Vance, and two silver bracelets by unknown Hopi artist using tobacco leaf hallmark.

HOMER VANCE

(Hopi, c. 1880s–1961)

Homer Vance, also known as "Home-Van-Tewa" and "Chief Corn Feather," was born at Shipaulovi. For a time in the 1920s, he worked in California as an actor in western films, but in 1927 Vance was employed as a silversmith at trader R. M. Bruchman's curio store in Winslow.

Vance married Sarah Lucy Coolidge, an Arapaho woman, and, in 1935, they opened Coolidge Indian Art Crafts in Hollywood, where he worked as manager and as silversmith. The store closed in 1938 when the Vances moved to her family home in Colorado Springs. In 1939, Vance demonstrated silversmithing in the Arizona Exhibit at the Golden Gate International Exposition in San Francisco. At some point in his career, he spent a year working as a silversmith at the Grand Canyon. Homer Vance died in 1961.

Vance's jewelry is incredibly rare, but he appears to have been an excellent craftsman. Much of his jewelry is likely unsigned, and it is unknown at what period he signed his work. For this reason, and possibly because he spent considerable time in California, his importance as an early Hopi silversmith has been obscured. His hallmark consisted of the initials HV with a crescent design, possibly representing the Sun Clan.

FRED PESHLAKAI

(NAVAJO, C. 1896–1974)

Fred Peshlakai, a son of Beshlagai Ithlinne, was born at Crystal, New Mexico, about 1896. As a boy, Fred learned to melt and hammer silver from his father, who at one time had a silver shop in Crystal and paid as many as ten men to help him with his work. In the early 1900s, his father quit silversmithing because of impaired eyesight, so Fred did not completely develop his craft until later. Fred left the reservation to pursue a number of different jobs, from cowboy to movie actor, but, by the late 1920s, he had returned to working silver. At Ganado in 1927, Fred married June Hubbard, a Navajo woman who bore him two daughters. Fred made jewelry at a curio store he owned in Gallup, but, in 1931, was hired as the first instructor of silversmithing at the Fort Wingate Indian School.

In the summer of 1934, Fred demonstrated silverwork for the New Mexico Exhibition at the Chicago World's Fair. He resigned from the Wingate school in 1935, afterward working for a variety of Indian shops, including Skiles Indian Store in Phoenix and Vaughn's Indian Store in Phoenix and Hollywood. According to John Adair, Fred was running a shop in 1940 at the popular tourist destination Olvera Street, near Union Station in Los Angeles. He operated not only the shop in Los Angeles but another at the Hotel El Escalante in Cedar City, Utah, in 1950.

Fred maintained his shop on Olvera Street until several years of failing health forced him to retire around 1970. He was admitted to a Los Angeles area hospital in early 1973, and later that same year returned to the Navajo reservation where his daughter, Dorothy, cared for him until his death in December 1974.

Fred Peshlakai is credited with being the first Navajo silversmith to sign his work. He told Arthur Woodward that before 1934 or 1935, "he stamped his wares with a small hogan as a trademark," but he sold the hogan stamp to one of his former students, Kenneth Begay. After that he started stamping his work with a capital FP superimposed over an arrow typically facing left.

1- Three items made by Fred Peshlakai (Navajo). Pin is unmarked, right ring is signed in interior, and left band ring is signed on exterior. *Courtesy Karen Sires.*

2- Cast pin at bottom by Fred Peshlakai (Navajo), top pin made by Fred or Frank Peshlakai (Navajo) signed F.P. on reverse. *Courtesy Karen Sires.*

3- Heavy bracelet with teardrop turquoise setting, signed F.P. on the reverse, made by Fred or Frank Peshlakai (Navajo). *Courtesy Karen Sires.*

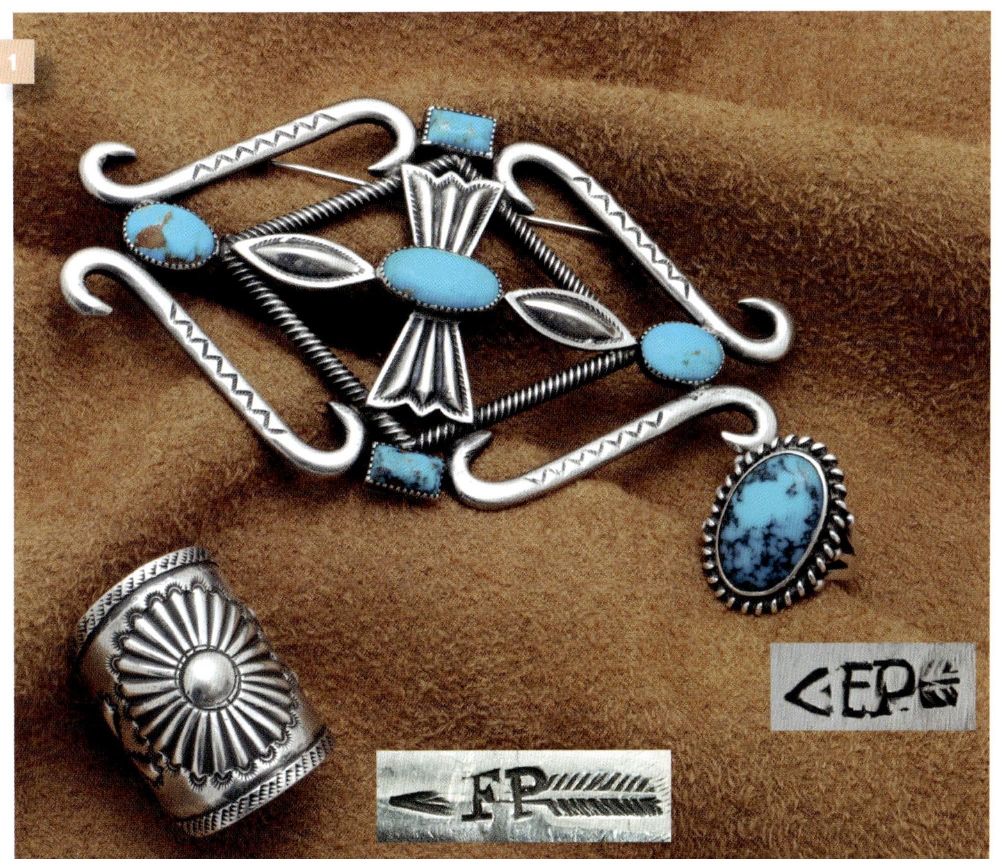

Photo postcard of Navajo silversmith, hand signed by Frank Peshlakai, c. 1930. *Authors' collection and Karen Sires.*

FRANK PESHLAKAI

(Navajo, 1903–1965)

Frank Peshlakai, also a son of Beshlagai Ithlinne, was the younger brother of Fred Peshlakai. Frank graduated from Albuquerque Indian School, and, in the early 1930s, he worked as a silversmith at Verkamp's Indian Store at the Grand Canyon. In 1934, he began to work for Babbitt Brothers in Flagstaff. He spent some time in Phoenix in 1935, and then ventured to Los Angeles by 1940, where he worked as a silversmith. It can only be assumed that he was working with his brother, Fred. Around 1945, Frank married Loris Ponzo, a Shoshone woman, and they had two daughters together. Frank remained in Los Angeles into the 1950s but relocated to Gallup by 1964; he passed away in December 1965.

Frank Peshlakai hallmarked his work with his full name in block capital letters or with F. PESHLAKAI using a small chisel to form the letters. Hallmarks using only the initials F.P. may be attributed to either Frank or Fred Peshlakai, but it may never be known which of the brothers used it more often.

Fred's obituary stated that he had taught silversmithing to Frank, and it is likely that Frank also worked with Fred in Los Angeles. Because of their long association, their work is similar in design and technique, sharing many qualities such as tasteful designs, the use of high-quality turquoise, twisted wire, and heavy-gauge silver. Consequently, their silverwork is difficult to tell apart. Confusion arises over the hallmarks the brothers used and may never be clarified.

JUAN DE DIOS

(ZUNI, 1882—AFTER 1940)

Juan De Dios, whose last name has been spelled a variety of ways including Dedios, Dideos, and Deleosa, was born in 1882 at Zuni Pueblo. He first appears in the U.S. Indian Census of 1928 as Juan De Dios, he was either a single man or a widower, and it does not appear that he ever fathered any children. Zuni trader John D. Kennedy in his book, *A Good Trade*, recalls De Dios was a diabetic amputee who spent a lot of time at his workbench. De Dios lived alone until about 1937 when he moved in with his niece, Ruth Simplicio, and her husband, Frank Calavaza. He was still alive and working as a silversmith in 1940 when the federal census was taken at Zuni; it is unknown when he actually passed away.

Though De Dios worked closely with C. G. Wallace, he also sold his work to other Zuni traders, including Wallace's brother, Robert, who owned Zuni Trading Post. In 1939, a cast bracelet with turquoise settings and a plain silver pin, both made by De Dios, won blue ribbons at the Gallup Inter-Tribal Ceremonial.

According to C. G. Wallace, Juan De Dios was one of five silversmiths at Zuni in 1918, and John Adair said De Dios was one of the oldest working silversmiths at the pueblo when he conducted his research. De Dios was knowledgeable in all forms of silverwork, but he learned the technique of casting from a Navajo and specialized in it during his career. He worked in the traditional way, hand-hammering coins for wrought work and melting them for cast work. He made many types of jewelry but is best known for bracelets, concho belts, and Knifewing pins.

1- Three cast pins, two Knifewing design and one Rainbow Man design by Juan De Dios (Zuni). Left Knifewing and Rainbow Man pins marked on back JD. *Courtesy Karen Sires.*

2- Unsigned silver bracelet made by Juan De Dios (Zuni) set with Blue Gem turquoise; with cast deer head appliqués on each side. *Courtesy Karen Sires.*

3- Tufa-cast bracelet with Lone Mountain turquoise stones made by Juan De Dios (Zuni) while working for C. G. Wallace, stamped with the Indian Arts and Crafts Board hallmark U.S.ZUNI 1. Made between the years 1938–1943.

Juan De Dios was one of the earliest Zuni silversmiths to sign his work, though he signed sporadically. As early as the 1920s, he stamped the initials JD using a small chisel. Some items attributed to De Dios are marked U.S.ZUNI 1 because C. G. Wallace submitted his work to the Indian Arts and Crafts Board for stamping under the government's silver program.

ETSITTY TSOSIE

(NAVAJO, C. 1880–1937)

Pieces by Etsitty Tsosie (Navajo), commonly known as Eskie Tsosie. Bracelet is made of square hand-drawn wire and set with hand-cut turquoise, it was purchased at Maisel's in 1938. Set of copper butterfly pins attached with chain. Bracelet, *authors' collection.* Pins *courtesy Karen Sires.*

Etsitty Tsosie, referred to by John Adair as Eskie Tsosie, was born about 1880 and resided near Naschitti on the Navajo reservation. In 1904, Etsitty Tsosie was among a group of Navajos demonstrating silver at the Louisiana Purchase Exposition in St. Louis. He also demonstrated silver at the Gallup Inter-Tribal Ceremonial in the 1930s, where many of his creations won prizes for excellent craftsmanship. He worked for C. G. Wallace and other traders in the Gallup area. His death in June 1937 made national headlines, and he was hailed as the "most famed of Navajo silversmiths," who "never ceased making beautiful jewelry." He used large and small versions of a hallmark of crossed arrows that appear to have been made using one arrow stamp applied twice, one across the other.

RALPH TAWANGYAWMA

(HOPI, 1894–1972)

This bracelet exhibits some of the most delicate work made by Ralph Tawangyawma (Hopi). *Courtesy Robert F. Farling.*

Ralph Tawangyawma was born in October 1894 in Oraibi, as Ralph Lomawyma. He was a boy in 1906 when the Oraibi Split occurred, and his family moved to the new village of Hotevilla. During his teen years, he and a cousin experimented with silversmithing, using whatever materials were available. As an adult, he moved down from the mesas and became a full-time silversmith. About 1936 and possibly at the time he acquired his social security number, he changed his last name to Tawangyawma. In Phoenix he worked for at least three shops: Vaughn's Indian Store, Ollie Kirkpatrick's Trading Post, and Fred Wilson's Indian Trading Post (also in the Salt Lake City location in 1939).

By 1945, Tawangyawma had moved to Tucson and within two years was working for William and Irene McDaniel, owners of the Santa Rita Indian Shop in downtown Tucson. He worked there for many years with his nephew, Allen Pooyouma.

Tawangyawma was living in Tombstone, Arizona, in 1962 and working at the Hopi House most days of the week, but on Wednesdays he traveled north to work at the Tucson branch. A 1963 advertisement for Hopi House claimed:

> That amazing... Hopi Indian who does such beautiful work in sterling silver, has made some exceptional roadrunner pins, tie tacks, earrings, sweater guards, and belt buckles. Each individually designed and handmade from start to finish! The least expensive piece is $4.00, the most costly $25.00. Ralph Tawangyawma is his name.

About 1964 Tawangyawma retired from full-time work and moved back to Hotevilla where he was involved with the traditional and religious society of the village, but occasionally made some jewelry. He died November 1972 on the Hopi mesas.

Tawangyawma's work is distinctive for its use of heavy-gauge silver and overall stamping, leaving little empty space, and he was one of the few Hopis who mastered the art of channel inlay. He started hallmarking his work early, probably in the 1930s, and signed his pieces with a heavy capital "H" for Hopi and a thundercloud with streaks of lightning emanating from both sides. He possessed at least two different thundercloud stamps, but often scratched his hallmark into the back of his work.

1

2

1- Four bracelets made by Ralph Tawangyawma (Hopi).

2- Ashtray, 1930s, by Ralph Tawangyawma (Hopi), measures 8" in diameter, hand-cut and polished turquoise nuggets from a Nevada mine.

3- Earrings, rings, and pin and earring set by Ralph Tawangyawma (Hopi). All hallmarks are scratched in, the ring is signed only with the raincloud mark.

4- Heavy silver bracelet utilizing carinated and twisted bands with an unusual central chain-link section, by Ralph Tawangyawma (Hopi).

5- Two bolos and a buckle with turquoise settings, a plain silver quail pin, and a bar pin with amethyst settings by Ralph Tawangyawma (Hopi). Buckle hallmark lacks "H" for Hopi.

MORRIS ROBINSON

(Hopi, 1901–1984)

Publicity photo of Morris Robinson (Hopi), 1933, in a Phoenix, Arizona, grocery store. Anglos often posed American Indians, from any tribe or culture, in Plains-style headdresses and attire to lend an air of authenticity. © *Bettmann/CORBIS.*

When Morris Robinson was a boy, his family was involved in the Oraibi Split of 1906 and moved to the new village of Bacavi. He was known by his Hopi name Tealanytewa until 1912, when he was given the first name of Morris, and, by 1930, he had adopted the last name of Robinson, though he referred to himself off and on as Morris Tealanytewa. At some point in his career, cards were printed that stated:

An original by Tealanytewa (MORRIS ROBINSON) famous Hopi Indian silversmith

Sterling Silver ... *Hand Wrought*

His creations have won many honors in World, State and County Fair,

Ceremonial and Museum exhibits, and have been sold in many foreign countries.

Each piece bears his mark—the snake for his clan and the H for Hopi

"There is kinship to genius in the possession of original art."

Robinson attended school on the mesas, then in 1920 attended Phoenix Indian School. By 1924 he resided with his cousin Grant Jenkins who taught him silversmithing skills. Robinson lived and worked in Phoenix as a silversmith, including at Skiles Indian Shop in the early 1930s, and married a Pima woman in 1934.

Remarkable appliqué bracelet, butterfly pin, and cow head ring, all with turquoise settings, by Morris Robinson (Hopi). *Courtesy Karen Sires.*

Advertisement for Fred Wilson's Indian Trading Post in Phoenix, 1938, presenting Hopi hand-wrought silver boxes in all sizes. The Hopi silver craftsman mentioned in the ad was Morris Robinson.

Silver dishes, pill boxes, and jigger utilizing typical tourist-style stamps of arrows and swastikas, by Morris Robinson (Hopi), 1930s.

Robinson was working at Vaughn's Indian Store in Phoenix when it was sold to Fred Wilson in 1936, and he continued to work for the new owner. In May 1938, Fred Wilson's Indian Trading Post ran two national ads advertising Hopi hand-wrought salad sets and lidded boxes by his "master silversmith." Though Robinson was not named specifically in these ads, the items shown are decorated with his personal silver stamps.

Late 1930s bracelet and *ketoh* ring by Morris Robinson (Hopi). *Courtesy Karen Sires.*

It is not known when Robinson ceased to work for Fred Wilson, but it could have been in the late 1940s. In 1954, he was working at McCormick Indian Arts and Crafts Center in Scottsdale, and, in 1958, was employed by Godber's in Phoenix. In October 1961, as Morris Tealanytewa, he worked with Harry Sakyesva at Sakyesva Jewelry in Scottsdale where they fashioned "Fine custom made Hopi overlay pendants, earrings, bracelets, rings and buckles, beautifully designed in turquoise settings completely made by two Hopi craftsmen." But by 1963, Sakyesva was in a hospital in Denver and the Scottsdale store was likely closed. This could have been the time that Robinson retired from Phoenix and returned to Bacavi where he helped his brothers tend their sheep. He brought his tools with him and made occasional pieces. Robinson passed away at Hopi in August 1984.

Robinson was capable of working in many different styles and techniques. He mastered sheet and ingot silver, copper, overlay style, and cast work as well as hand-wrought boxes, bowls, vessels, and flatware. His early work showed well-designed decoration, and sometimes he incorporated elegant repoussé. He often made subtle designs of butterflies or dragonflies by the way he positioned his stamps, which he handmade from old files.

Robinson was marking his work by the early 1930s, possibly by 1931. His mark included both a snake and a capitol "H" for Hopi. There were two versions of the snake mark: a flat thin one with eyes in the head and a thicker one in profile with four segments for rattles. It seems he used both marks concurrently on his earlier work, but by time he was making modern-design silver, only the thin snake hallmark was used.

1- Dragonfly, butterfly, and bar pins, all made by Morris Robinson (Hopi). All items marked with snake and "H" except for dragonfly pin marked with FW shop mark used by Fred Wilson's Indian Trading Post.

2- Three bracelets and *ketoh* ring made by Morris Robinson (Hopi). Butterfly bracelet inlaid with settings likely bought wholesale and not cut by Robinson. Ring is marked with Fred Wilson's Indian Trading Post FW shop mark.

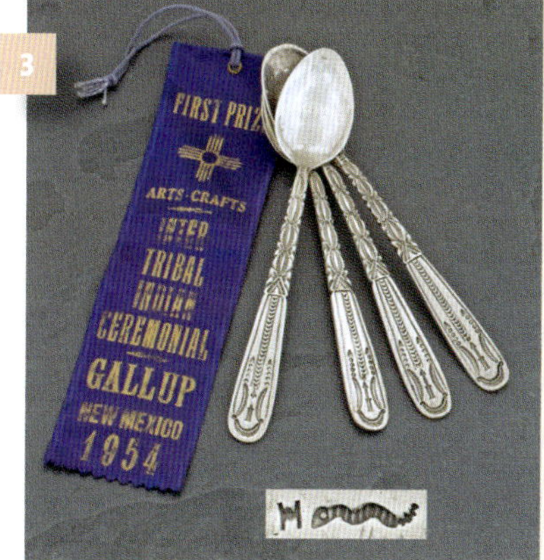

3- Set of hand-wrought teaspoons, by Morris Robinson (Hopi), which won First Prize ribbon at the 1954 Gallup Inter-Tribal Indian Ceremonial.

4- Modern-design pieces, c. 1950–1960, by Morris Robinson (Hopi), utilizing little or no stamp work. Likely influenced by White Hogan designs.

5- Dragonfly pendant made by Morris Robinson (Hopi). Two side pieces were added by Fred Peshlakai (Navajo) at a later date to create a necklace. *Private collection.*

DA-PAH

(Navajo, 1895–1977)

One Navajo silversmith, who was fairly well known and prominent in the 1930s, has been all but forgotten because little of his work was signed. He was known as Da-Pah, and one of the most circulated postcards of the tourist era shows him making silver using "primitive tools" in his hogan at Coolidge, New Mexico, where he and his family lived at B. I. Staples's Crafts del Navajo trading post on Route 66 east of Gallup.

In 1930, when Staples assembled a delegation of Navajos to travel through the eastern states, he chose Da-Pah to demonstrate silversmithing. They traveled for three months in the winter, visiting cities including Washington, D.C., Chicago, and New York. Staples gave presentations while the Indians demonstrated their crafts and sang traditional songs. These winter tours would last until Staples's death in 1938.

During one of these trips, Da-Pah became acquainted with the owners of the Indian Plaza, a curio shop in Charlemont, Massachusetts, on the historic Mohawk Trail. Starting in the summer of 1934, he and his family were employed at Indian Plaza, and Da-Pah continued to work there every summer until about 1960. When Da-Pah applied for his social security number in the 1930s, he adopted the first name of James and was sometimes referred to as Jimmy Dapah.

Da-Pah passed away in 1977 at the age of eighty-two near Continental Divide, New Mexico, not far from Staples's original Crafts del Navajo trading post. He was an excellent silversmith, whose work featured high-quality turquoise set on hand-hammered silver, and when he signed, which was infrequent, he would hand-etch his name.

126 NAVAJO INDIAN SILVERSMITH PLYING HIS TRADE

NAVAJO INDIANS AT WORK, INDIAN PLAZA, MOHAWK TRAIL, CHARLEMONT, MASS.

1- Da-Pah, Navajo Indian silversmith at Indian Plaza, Mohawk Trail, Charlemont, Massachusetts. He was employed there during the summers from 1934 until at least 1964.

2- Bracelet with nine oval turquoise stones, c. 1930. DAPAH is chiseled on the underside. Da-Pah was a Navajo silversmith who worked for Berton I. Staples at Coolidge, New Mexico, until 1938.

3- Postcards showing Da-Pah (Navajo) working silver, 1930s, left in his hogan at Coolidge, New Mexico, and right at Indian Plaza in Charlemont, Massachusetts.

AWA TSIREH

(San Ildefonso, 1898–1955)

The most celebrated silversmith to work at Garden of the Gods Trading Post was Awa Tsireh (Alfonso Roybal) from San Ildefonso Pueblo. He gained fame as an easel artist in the 1920s with a show in Chicago, and by the 1930s his paintings became increasingly sought after.

About 1920, Awa Tsireh married a woman from the village, and the following year she gave birth to a son, but mother and child died soon thereafter. This loss affected the artist greatly, and, as he moved back to his parents' home, he took solace in his artwork and never remarried.

1- December 14, 1931, photo of Awa Tsireh (San Ildefonso) in New York to exhibit paintings at the Exposition of Indian Tribal Arts at Grand Central Galleries. © *Bettmann/ CORBIS.*

2- Four oversized silver pins by Awa Tsireh (San Ildefonso). The largest is the roadrunner (5" wide); the skunk, thunderbird, and feather pins are somewhat smaller. All marked AWA TSIREH and include Garden of the Gods Trading Post shop marks.

3- Heavy silver bracelet with stamp and file work by Awa Tsireh (San Ildefonso), made while working at Garden of the Gods Trading Post.

It is not known when or from whom Awa Tsireh learned silversmithing, but, by 1931, he was described in newspaper articles as a painter and "a silversmith and a dancer." John Adair reported in his book that Awa Tsireh was one of three men in San Ildefonso who worked silver and that he made pieces in his studio for the tourists who would visit the pueblo.

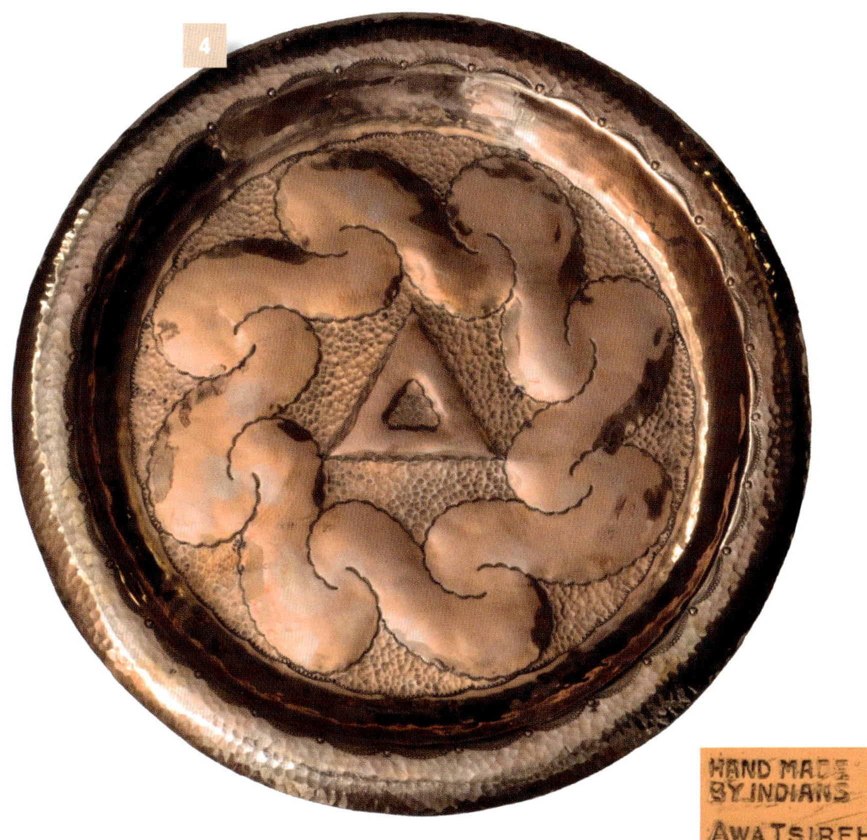

4- Heavy copper tray (12" dia.) with subtle repoussé work by Awa Tsireh (San Ildefonso), made while he was at Garden of the Gods Trading Post. When fashioned by skilled smiths copper could achieve beautiful results, and many talented Indian artists used copper as a medium.

Awa Tsireh's association with Garden of the Gods Trading Post had begun by 1930. Early advertising postcards from about that time depicted Awa Tsireh in the Colorado Springs area dressed in Plains-style attire. The 1933 city directory for Colorado Springs lists Awa Tsireh as a silversmith at Garden of the Gods Trading Company; as did the 1938 edition, when his younger brother, Ralph, also worked as a silversmith at the trading post.

Awa Tsireh was employed at Garden of the Gods Trading Post for at least two decades. His sister, Santana Martinez, recalled later that "during the summer during the thirties and forties he used to go to a shop in Colorado Springs and do his paintings and silverwork there" (Seymour, *When the Rainbow Touches Down*).

5- Photo postcard of Awa Tsireh (San Ildefonso) attired in Plains-style clothing, c. 1930, Colorado Springs.

6- Aluminum tray (10.5" dia.) by Awa Tsireh (San Ildefonso), hand-crimped piecrust rim, finely stamped depiction of Knifewing figure. Marked AWA TSIREH with Garden of the Gods Trading Post shop marks. This piece shows his metalwork was as precise as his paintings.

The Hutchinson, Kansas, *News-Herald* dated June 26, 1938, while reporting on the impending nuptials of a local couple, exclaimed in an article:

Spell it Awa Tsireh—pronounce is A-Wa Si-dy! Whoever he is, he's the Indian silversmith responsible for that symbolical silver plate which Elizabeth and Joe, to wed today, will give choice place in their household. Of about luncheon size, the plate center is beaten and etched with a god to watch over them, and filled in about and on the rim with emblems of wisdom, constancy, love and happiness. There is no other plate like it and there won't be for the famous "Awa Sidy" never duplicates. Of New Mexico originally, he's now collaborating with Charles E. Strausenback in a museum at the Garden of the Gods. The gorgeous silver bracelets which Elizabeth often wears are his work.

Though his production of paintings and silverwork slowed after the war, Awa Tsireh continued to work. In 1954 he was awarded the French government's Ordre des Palmes Académiques for "distinguished contributions to education or culture" along with twelve other Indian artists including Ambrose Roanhorse and Fred Kabotie.

Awa Tsireh died tragically from exposure on the outskirts of San Ildefonso on March 29, 1955. He was memorialized a few months later by the Museum of New Mexico in Santa Fe with an exhibit of forty-three examples of his paintings.

Awa Tsireh is well regarded as a master of Pueblo painting. He was remembered as a quiet man of slight build, with a good sense of humor, who wore his hair in the long braids of his pueblo's tradition. His paintings were meticulously and precisely drawn and are well represented in major American art museum collections including the Smithsonian Institution.

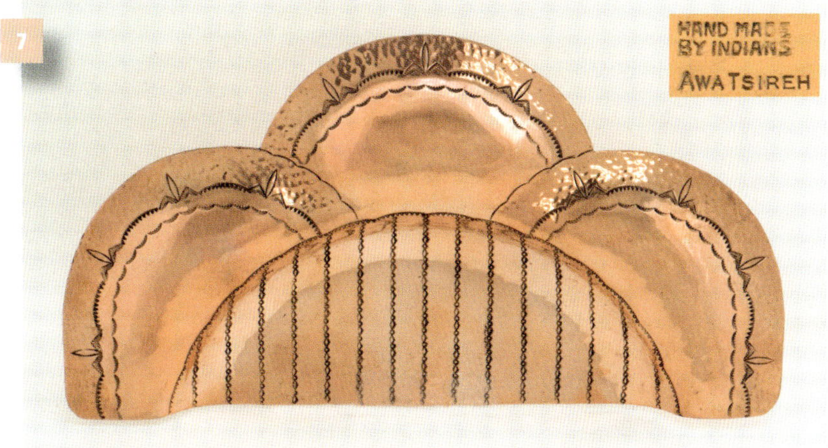

7- Pueblo cloud design copper crumb tray (10" wide) by Awa Tsireh (San Ildefonso). Less expensive than silver, copper was often used as a teaching or practice material, but also highly collectible from the 1920s to the 1950s and in demand for wearable and decorative items.

8- Curio-type items made by Awa Tsireh (San Ildefonso). Sugar spoon, matchbook holder, pin, turtle pill box, and "V" for Victory pin, early 1940s. All pieces are marked AWA TSIREH and, except for the round pin, also marked with Garden of the Gods Trading Post shop marks.

9- Photo postcard of Awa Tsireh (San Ildefonso) at Manitou, Colorado.

Unfortunately, his silverwork was rarely collected by the same institutions, and it is now found mainly in private collections. What has been written about Awa Tsireh's paintings is also true of his metalwork: that he was precise and meticulous and a master artist. He worked not only in the medium of silver but also copper, nickel silver, and at least once in aluminum. Though he traveled fairly often, especially in summer, he always made the village of San Ildefonso his home.

Awa Tsireh made a variety of forms during his silversmithing career, including bracelets, pins, rings, trays, bowls, and concho belts. He signed his work AWA TSIREH and most often with one of Garden of the Gods shop marks such as SOLID SILVER. Pieces that were signed just with his name were likely made at his studio in the pueblo. Items bearing shop marks from Garden of the Gods Trading Post, but lacking the hallmark for Awa Tsireh, are not of the same quality as his signed pieces. Consequently, only those pieces bearing his hallmark can be credited as his work.

HORACE IULE

(Zuni, 1899–1978)

Horace Iule attended Phoenix Indian School in the early 1920s and was trained as a blacksmith. Upon his return to Zuni, he was not able to find sufficient work, so his father—whose father was one of the earliest silversmiths at Zuni—taught him silversmithing. By 1924, Iule was skilled enough to take a position teaching silversmithing at Zuni Day School, where he remained until the late 1930s.

Iule was able to make a living solely from his silversmithing skills, and in the late 1930s, he was regarded as one of the best silversmiths in the village. His training as a blacksmith allowed him to fabricate tools for his own use as well as for sale to other silversmiths. One of the most versatile smiths, he could make wrought spoons, ashtrays, or row bracelets hammered from ingots; he cut and polished turquoise by hand; and he was one of the few Zunis who made large hand-hammered pieces with stamped decorations. Yet Horace Iule is best known for his cast pieces.

It was standard practice at Zuni and around Gallup for traders to consign silver and turquoise to the silversmiths, and when the finished goods were brought back to the trader, the silversmith would be paid only for his labor; many times payment would be made in store credit only. Becoming disenchanted with this system, Iule ventured to Gallup where he purchased his own silver and turquoise and could then sell the finished product to whomever he chose.

It appears Iule began signing his work H. IULE after World War II and that signed pieces were almost exclusively done by casting. His most commonly made designs were Knifewing figures and heavy crosses with turquoise settings. Horace Iule passed away at Zuni in 1978, but his family continues to use his molds to make crosses; these pieces are signed with the family members' first initial and IULE.

1

2

3

1- Frasher's postcard of Horace Iule (Zuni), c. 1930.

2- Photo of Horace Iule (Zuni) taken in his home, c. 1970.

3- Ranger buckle set by Horace Iule (Zuni), c. 1950, includes buckle, two keepers, and tip. The turquoise stones are cut and polished by hand and set in tiny serrated bezels. Buckle was cast; keepers and tip were made from sheet silver. Buckle and tip marked H.IULE.

4- Two cross pendants and Knifewing design pin made by Horace Iule (Zuni). Pendants on left, *authors' collection.* Pin on right, *courtesy Madeleine Nash.*

5- Cast squash blossom necklace made by Horace Iule (Zuni). *Private collection.*

Ike Wilson

(Navajo, c.1901–1942)

Isaac "Ike" Wilson was born into a family of silversmiths. His grandfather was said to be the first Navajo silversmith to move to the Zuni area around 1920, where, residing south of Gallup, he worked for trader Charles Kelsey. Ike married Katherine, the sister of silversmith Charlie Bitsui and, settling near Zuni, they both became employed by Kelsey Trading Company around 1925. By the early 1930s, Ike was already a well-known silversmith in the region. Katherine was a skilled silversmith in her own right and, in 1939, both Ike and "Mrs. Ike Wilson" won multiple awards at Gallup Inter-Tribal Ceremonial for their silverwork. Ike won three awards for concho belts and Katherine won for a bracelet, buttons, a pin, and strings of turquoise beads. John Adair reported in the late 1930s that Ike and Katherine had "an income of close to $2000 a year from their silver," whereas the average income of Navajo silversmiths was $383 a year.

Ike met a tragic death in the summer of 1942, when Katherine accidentally shot him in their home. Ike was well regarded as one of the foremost Navajo silversmiths at the time of his death and was credited with innovations and developments in Navajo silversmithing that had advanced the art. It was reported at the time of his death that Ike had worked for Kelsey Trading Company for seventeen years, but he also did work for C. G. Wallace, John Kennedy Sr., and others.

After Ike's death, Katherine continued to work silver, and it has been stated that she used her husband's hallmark on her own work. In an ad for Tanner's Indian Arts in the Winter 1976 issue of *American Indian Art* magazine, a sketch of Katherine's bow and arrow hallmark was displayed. This drawing confirms that the bow and arrow mark belonged to Ike Wilson. This mark has been erroneously assigned to Austin Wilson since the early 1980s. According to trader John Kennedy Sr., Ike and Austin were not related, not even by clan. After her long career, Katherine Wilson passed away near Zuni in 1985.

Concho belt made before 1942 by Ike Wilson (Navajo). *Courtesy White collection.*

Pre-1942 bracelet and ring by Navajo silversmith Ike Wilson. *Courtesy Karen Sires.*

Hand-hammered ingot silver, split-shank bracelet with rectangular Blue Gem setting, 1930s, by Ike Wilson (Navajo).

AUSTIN WILSON

(NAVAJO, C.1901–1976)

Navajo silversmith Austin Wilson was born around Leupp, Arizona. He married a woman named either Gennepth or Gapa and, by 1935, was working as a silversmith in the Zuni area. He worked for a variety of traders including C. G. Wallace, Robert Wallace, John Kennedy Sr., and also George Rummage in the 1950s. Austin Wilson made at least one set of flatware in 1939 that won a blue ribbon at Gallup Inter-Tribal Ceremonial, and he was still working in 1959, when he won an award for a bracelet with stones at the ceremonial. He resided for most of his life between Gallup and Zuni and passed away December 1976. Even though he has been credited with many pieces marked with a bow and arrow, it is more likely Austin Wilson used a tomahawk hallmark, or possibly no mark at all.

Knifewing inlaid pin with tomahawk hallmark. This mark usually appears on silverwork incorporating Zuni inlay. The tomahawk hallmark was probably used by Navajo silversmith Austin Wilson, who worked for C. G. Wallace and other Zuni traders. *Photo by Karen Sires, courtesy Karen Sires.*

HUNT BROTHERS OF ACOMA

CLYDE HUNT (C. 1900–1972)
WAYNE HENRY "WOLF ROBE" HUNT (C. 1902–1977)
WILBERT HUNT (C. 1906–2007)

Postcard of Clyde Sunny Skies Hunt (left) and his brother, Wayne Wolf Robe Hunt (Acoma), displaying their handmade jewelry at Clyde's War Bonnet Shop in Albuquerque, late 1930s.

Three brothers from Acoma Pueblo—Clyde, Wayne, and Wilbert Hunt—made names for themselves as well-known silversmiths and entertainers. Before 1920, the family, headed by Edward Hunt, known as "Chief Big Snake," moved from Acoma to the Albuquerque area where they were known for performing Indian dances and songs. The Hunt family toured Europe from 1927 to 1928 when the Smithsonian Institution sponsored them as part of an educational program.

The oldest of the three brothers, Clyde (or Claudio) Hunt was the first to learn silversmithing while working for Maisel's. He worked in Albuquerque curio shops until 1934 when he opened his own jewelry business called the War Bonnet, earning a reputation for being one of the first American Indians to own a jewelry shop in Albuquerque. John Adair reported that, in 1940, Clyde's shop employed two silversmiths and that Clyde himself had taken several prizes at Gallup Ceremonial. He operated the business in Albuquerque until 1941, and then moved it to Carlsbad, New Mexico. Wearing a Plains-style headdress and beating a Pueblo drum, "Chief Sunny Skies," as he became known, would entertain visitors to his shop with traditional dances, songs, and stories. Clyde would run the War Bonnet in Carlsbad until his death in January 1972. Clyde's jewelry is relatively rare, possibly because he never used a hallmark, preferring to hand-etch his work with a variation of "Hand Made by Sunny Skies Acoma Ind." During the time Clyde had his shop in Albuquerque, he taught his brothers Wayne and Wilbert to make silver.

1- Silver bracelet set with turquoise by Clyde Hunt (Acoma), hand-engraved on reverse, "Hand Made by Chief Sunny Skies Acoma Ind, New Mexico."

2- Business card for Catoosa Indian Trading Post, owned and operated by Wolf Robe Hunt (Acoma).

3- Pendant made by Wolf Robe Hunt (Acoma).

The most acclaimed of the Hunt brothers was Wayne Henry "Wolf Robe" Hunt, who was known as Henry through the 1930s. He attended public high school and lived in Albuquerque until 1938, when he and his family settled in Tulsa, Oklahoma. He partnered with his brother-in-law Hugh Davis to open the Catoosa Indian Trading Post on Route 66. Wolf Robe would spend his career dressing in Plains Indian attire and making silver jewelry, leather crafts, and paintings; touring the country and occasionally Europe; and presenting educational programs including Pueblo dances. He exhibited at Gallup Inter-Tribal Ceremonial every August starting in the 1930s and won many awards, especially for his leather work. He taught silversmithing classes at the Philbrook Art Center in Tulsa and, in 1963, illustrated and co-authored with Helen Rushmore the folklore book *The Dancing Horses of Acoma*. Wolf Robe Hunt died after a brief illness in a Tulsa hospital in December 1977. He worked silver most of his adult life and made a large quantity of signed pieces. He used WOLF-ROBE as a hallmark of which there are two versions—one with a hyphen and one without—and made many pieces of tourist-style jewelry with plentiful stamp work and good quality stones. One of his signature styles was a cast silver snake bracelet with turquoise set in the terminals, one terminal depicting the snake's head and the other the rattles.

The youngest and least well known of the Hunt brothers was Wilbert. He lived with his parents in Albuquerque and learned to make silver while working for his brother Clyde in the late 1930s. Wilbert was known as "Blue Sky Eagle," and in 1939 was the proprietor of Blue Sky Eagle Curios in Albuquerque. He enlisted in the Army in 1942, serving in Germany during the war; upon his return to Albuquerque, he was hired by Bell Trading Post where he worked as a silversmith. In 1947, he designed Bell's line of dime-store copper and nickel jewelry called "Redskin Maid." Wilbert made jewelry well into his nineties and died in Albuquerque in 2007. His handmade jewelry is unidentified since it appears he never used a hallmark.

Cast snake bracelet, two sets of earrings, twist bracelet, and watch bracelet, all made by Wolf Robe Hunt (Acoma).

PAUL SAUFKIE

(Hopi, 1904–1998)

Paul Saufkie (Hopi) working on bracelet while demonstrating silver at the M. H. deYoung Memorial Museum in San Francisco, November 1953.

Paul Saufkie (Hopi) in San Francisco, November 1953. He, Fred and Alice Kabotie, along with their son, Michael, traveled there for a show at the M. H. deYoung Memorial Museum.

One of the most influential silversmiths who lived and worked on the Hopi mesas, Paul Saufkie was born in Shungopavi in 1904. In his early teens, Saufkie attended Phoenix Indian School. He learned silversmithing from his father Andrew Humiquaptewa, who was trained in blacksmithing at Carlisle Indian School. After marriage to his second wife, their first son, Lawrence, was born February 10, 1934.

Saufkie worked for the Fred Harvey Company at the Grand Canyon during the summer months, demonstrating silversmithing at least from 1934 to 1937; during the other months, he worked at Vaughn's Indian Store in Phoenix. Returning to Shungopavi, he became one the leading silversmiths on the mesas before World War II and opened his own shop on the outskirts of the village, but the limited number of visitors to the mesas provided few opportunities to sell his work.

Saufkie found an outlet in Flagstaff at the Museum of Northern Arizona's Hopi Craftsman Exhibition and often demonstrated silversmithing there from 1938 onward. That same year, Mary-Russell Colton began her program to make Hopi silver more distinctive and unique, and Saufkie was the biggest supporter of the program and the new designs. His association with the museum would last throughout his career.

Alfred Whiting made a survey of Hopi crafts for the Indian Arts and Crafts Board in 1941 and noted Saufkie was "perhaps the only real smith on the reservation today" and that he was "loaded with orders and what is most important, is having a strong influence upon other smiths, especially the younger ones." Saufkie was making a variety of styles: some were typical tourist designs, some were his original ideas, and others used the new patterns from MNA. Whiting also observed that Saufkie was in Salt Lake City the winter of 1941–1942, where he was working at Thompson's Indian Trading Post, but that he would return to the reservation in the summer.

Saufkie and his brother-in-law, Fred Kabotie, in 1947, organized silversmithing classes for Hopi veterans of World War II under the G.I. Bill of Rights. Saufkie was the technical instructor, teaching the students everything from making their own stamping dies, to melting and hammering silver slugs and making tufa molds, to the techniques of appliqué, overlay, and inlay.

Kabotie, Saufkie, and some of the students from the first class formed the Hopi Silvercraft Cooperative Guild in 1949 at Oraibi, as a sales outlet and showroom and as a supplier of materials and workshop space for the graduates.

Saufkie worked with the Hopi Guild and also from his Shungopavi shop for many years doing silverwork and weaving ceremonial textiles. His silverwork is typically of heavy gauge, usually utilizes hand-hammered silver with overlay and appliqué work, and often incorporates turquoise as a setting or inlaid in traditional Hopi patterns. He continued to exhibit at shows around the Southwest; in 1992, he was an exhibitor at Santa Fe Indian Market showing jewelry and weavings. He received the Arizona Indian Living Treasure Award in 1991 and retired by 1993. Saufkie passed away in his home village of Shungopavi in January 1998, but his contribution to Hopi silver lives on.

Saufkie may not have used a hallmark before the G.I. Bill classes started in 1947. Some of his pieces from the first class bear only his Hopi Trademark Sunface hallmark; later it would be joined by the angular snow cloud that is Saufkie's personal mark. This mark consists of a hat-shaped stamp with three, four, or five boxes below signifying falling snow.

1- Bracelet and ring, 1947–1949, by Paul Saufkie (Hopi), marked only with his veterans' class Sunface trademark stamp. The silver was cast into ingots and then hand-hammered to shape. Bracelet published in July 1950 issue of *Arizona Highways*.

2- Overlay bolo with corn plant design by Paul Saufkie (Hopi), c. 1970, signed with Saufkie's snow cloud mark and a later version of the Hopi Guild Sunface mark.

3- Overlay pendant and pin by Paul Saufkie (Hopi), early 1950s, signed with Saufkie's Hopi Guild trademark and his snow cloud hallmark.

4- Overlay bracelet by Paul Saufkie (Hopi), made November 1953 as a gift to Ruth and Charles Elkus for arranging the show at the M. H. deYoung Memorial Museum in San Francisco. CAS 0370-1555. *Courtesy California Academy of Sciences, Ruth and Charles deYoung Elkus Collection.*

DAViD TALiMAN

(Navajo, 1901–1967)

David Taliman was originally from Ganado but married a woman from Santa Clara Pueblo, where they made their home. In 1930, Taliman was working as a silversmith at Julius Gans's Southwest Arts and Crafts in Santa Fe, where he had learned his craft. Later, he was employed by Maisel's in Albuquerque off and on for about eighteen years. In 1940, he was recruited by Trans-Continental Western Airlines (TWA) to travel with the planes across the country and to demonstrate jewelry making in the different cities where TWA had stops; he worked under the name Hosteen Nez. For about eight years, he worked for the Wooden Indian Trading Post in Los Alamos and Rinconada, and, in 1965, he was employed part-time at the Shalako Shop in Los Alamos. At some point he must have worked at Garden of the Gods Trading Post because some of his pieces are marked with SOLID SILVER HAND MADE BY INDIANS. He used a personal hallmark of D.TALIMAN. David Taliman passed away in Santa Fe in November 1967.

Silver bolo slide with large turquoise setting made by David Taliman (Navajo). It appears Taliman's hallmark was stamped over the personal mark of Mark Chee (Navajo).

Silver bracelet made by David Taliman (Navajo) while working at Garden of the Gods Trading Post. *Courtesy Karen Sires.*

Copper Sunface bracelet and concho belt, and silver concho belt with turquoise sets, both made by David Taliman (Navajo). Copper set, *authors' collection.* Silver belt, *courtesy White collection.*

AMBROSE ROANHORSE

(Navajo, c.1904–1982)

Ambrose Roanhorse was one of the most influential Navajo silversmiths of his time. Born near Ganado, he started learning silverwork at the age of nine by helping his grandfather. Roanhorse, who went by the name of Roans until 1939, attended reservation schools before enrolling in the Haskell Institute at Lawrence, Kansas.

Making his way back to the Southwest after graduation, he married a Navajo weaver and, about 1928, they settled in Santa Fe where Roanhorse was hired to work at Southwest Arts and Crafts as a silversmith. Owner Julius Gans would later declare that Roanhorse "learned his trade in our shop." When silversmithing classes began at the Santa Fe Indian School, Roanhorse was hired as the first instructor for the 1931–1932 term, and he continued living on the grounds and teaching there through the spring of 1939.

Roanhorse participated in the discussions of silver standards proposed by the Indian Arts and Crafts Board. After the government program was established in 1938, Roanhorse became Kenneth Chapman's assistant, inspecting the jewelry and applying the identification stamp.

In June 1939, Roanhorse was selected as director of a new craft program and relocated to its headquarters at Fort Wingate. Roanhorse's responsibilities included distributing supplies to craftsmen and picking up their completed work to be sold by the guild. In 1941, the guild expanded to benefit the entire tribe and became the Navajo Arts and Crafts Guild, for which Roanhorse served as assistant manager for a few years.

During this time, Roanhorse was busy with other responsibilities and therefore made little silver of his own, even as his reputation as a master silversmith grew. He traveled to Gallup to judge the entries at the Inter-Tribal Ceremonial and, in 1941, he contributed items and attended the opening of an exhibit of Indian art at the Museum of Modern Art in New York City.

In 1954, Roanhorse was one of thirteen Indians honored by the French government, when he was awarded with the Ordre des Palmes Académiques, the French Republic's award for his distinguished achievements in silverwork. By 1956, his schedule had eased enough so that Roanhorse could enter a concho belt in the Gallup Ceremonial that took a First Place ribbon. By this time, he had already won many awards for his hand-wrought work.

Roanhorse retired from the Bureau of Indian Affairs in 1960 after thirty years of service.

He continued to teach silversmithing at various venues and, through the 1960s, he contributed to various programs on the reservation including the Office of Navajo Economic Opportunity. Roanhorse passed away in 1982, leaving as his greatest legacy the many fine craftsmen who learned directly from him or indirectly from one of his former students, and who benefited from the programs and institutions he helped put into place.

Although many pieces of Roanhorse's work do not bear his hallmark of a stick horse whose legs form the initials AR, they are distinctive by the bold simple design and the high quality of workmanship. His work should not be confused with that of Ambrose Lincoln, who used an entirely different hallmark.

1- Bracelet by Ambrose Roanhorse (Navajo), signed with his hallmark of a stick horse whose legs form the initials AR. *Courtesy Karen Sires.*

2- Silver bracelet with chrysocolla setting by Ambrose Roanhorse, 1955. CAS 0370-1576. *Courtesy California Academy of Sciences, Ruth and Charles deYoung Elkus Collection.*

Sylvester Santiago (Zuni, 1911–1993) | Frieda Santiago (Hopi, 1913–1989)

Sylvester Santiago most likely learned to work silver at Maisel's in Albuquerque, where he was employed in 1930. He married Frieda Seyowma, a Hopi woman from Kykotsmovi, in 1933. Frieda learned silversmithing techniques by watching her relative, Willie Coin. Sylvester worked as a silversmith at a variety of stores: Vaughn's Indian Store in Phoenix in 1935; Vaughn's in Williams in 1940; at several shops in Salt Lake City during the war and the late 1940s, including Thompson Indian Trading Post; and in the 1950s in Phoenix at Indian School Trading Post. He also worked from his residence where Frieda helped with the silversmithing.

Margaret Wright reports in *Hopi Silver* that Frieda quit because of impaired eyesight about 1964. Frieda helped Sylvester during his career, especially when he worked on his own. A hallmark of an ear of corn with a capital letter "Z" for Zuni was undoubtedly the personal mark of Sylvester and was probably shared with Frieda. The jewelry they supplied to dealers was unique, favoring delicate shadowbox designs with small turquoise settings, as well as cast pieces—pins, bracelets, earrings, and bolos—with a running roadrunner design. They both passed away while residing in Phoenix.

Necklace and pin by Sylvester Santiago (Zuni) and his wife, Frieda Santiago (Hopi).

Lewis Lomay

(Hopi, 1913–1996)

Lewis Lomay, born at Oraibi as Lewis Lomayesva, learned to draw while attending school in the early 1920s. Lomay was enrolled about 1929 at the Albuquerque Indian School where he took some art classes; after three years, he left to attend Dorothy Dunn's art class at the Santa Fe Indian School. Four months later, he switched to Ambrose Roanhorse's silversmithing class.

For the fall term of 1934, after his return to Santa Fe from Hopi, Lomay found it was too late for him to enroll at school. He hired on at the Thunderbird Shop, painting pictures to be sold in the store. He worked for about a dollar a day, but owner Frank Patania would buy lunch and pay the rent on an apartment for him and Waldo Mootzka, Lomay's Hopi friend and co-worker.

About a year later, Patania discovered that Lomay could do silverwork. Frank gave him a bench and tools in the back room and told him to put away his brushes. Lomay learned fine jewelry techniques and modern designs from Patania. In 1937, Lomay married a woman from San Juan Pueblo, and the same year Patania opened his second shop in Tucson. Lomay would then alternate between living in Tucson in the winter and Santa Fe in the summer. About 1938, he shortened his last name from Lomayesva to Lomay because the new name was easier to pronounce.

In 1942, Lomay quit his job and went to work in an aircraft plant. After the war, he returned to Santa Fe and opened the Hopi Indian Silver Shop in 1946. But the market for jewelry was slow, so he closed the shop and worked as a house painter while he continued to make jewelry in his spare time from a studio in his home. Lomay started to enter pieces in fairs and exhibits and quickly built a reputation as a master of his craft and, by 1947, he was winning multiple awards whenever he entered.

Over the next decade, his jewelry was represented by Santa Fe dealers, such as the Shop of the Rainbow Man, and was displayed at Under the Portal at the First National Bank of Santa Fe on the plaza, whose 1954 ad stated:

> At the New Mexico State Fair Lewis Lomay again proved that he is one of the few present-day masters of the art and craft of silver-smithing by walking away with a fist full of prizes including the first, second and third prizes in rings, earrings, and brooches with settings... Here is silverwork at its best; carefully and painstakingly made, yet with a fresh and imaginative beauty that is a pleasure to see.

His jewelry continued to win awards and, at the Annual Scottsdale National Indian Arts Exhibition in 1976, his work was demanding top dollar. By this time he was able to devote himself to full-time silversmithing. Lewis Lomay continued to work until his death on August 6, 1996, in Santa Fe.

Over his career Lomay worked in silver and gold with various stone settings. His work is signed a variety of ways: one of his first hallmarks is a capital "L" inside a Zia sun symbol, but his main hallmark was that of a curved snake. Some of his pieces are signed with the snake and LOMAY SILVER SANTA FE, and by the 1970s, he signed with the snake and LL.

Three-dimensional flower spray pin set with turquoise and coral (4" high), influenced by Patania designs, made by Lewis Lomay (Hopi).

Three bracelets and a pin, all marked with "L" inside Zia sun hallmark used by Lewis Lomay (Hopi).

Two pins and two bolo ties in various design techniques by Lewis Lomay (Hopi).

Buckle and cast pin marked LOMAY SILVER SANTA FE; earrings marked L.L. with snake mark; all by Lewis Lomay (Hopi).

1970s modern-design earrings and earlier ring by Lewis Lomay (Hopi). *Courtesy Karen Sires.*

KENNETH BEGAY

(NAVAJO, 1913–1977)

From Steamboat Canyon, Arizona, Kenneth Begay attended the school at Crystal, New Mexico, then enrolled at Fort Wingate Indian School, where he learned silversmithing from Fred Peshlakai in the early 1930s. During the summers between school terms, he would work demonstrating silver in national parks: Bryce Canyon, Zion National Monument, and the north rim of the Grand Canyon.

After school, Begay moved to Flagstaff in 1937, married a woman from Window Rock, and worked as a silversmith for Babbitt Brothers, making traditional jewelry until 1946. By 1940, his cousin, Allen Kee, had joined him in Flagstaff and, in 1946, both men partnered with John Bonnell to start the White Hogan.

White Hogan gave Begay the freedom to break out from the traditional designs practiced by most Navajo silversmiths at the time. His designs quickly became less cluttered and more sophisticated, and, by 1950, he was winning countless awards at fairs and exhibits in the Southwest.

In 1964, Begay left White Hogan to manage the Cameron branch of the Navajo Arts and Crafts Guild; then, in 1969, he became the first instructor of silversmithing at Navajo Community College. He remained there until his retirement and returned to Steamboat Canyon in 1972, working from his home until his death on December 23, 1977. In 2000, Kenneth Begay was posthumously bestowed the Lifetime Achievement Award from Southwest Association for Indian Arts (SWAIA), the organization that runs Indian Market in Santa Fe.

Early in his career, Begay made traditional Navajo-style jewelry for the national parks and curio shops. These pieces were not signed; as Begay stated in Carl Rosnek and Joseph Stacey's *Skystone and Silver*, "I began marking my jewelry in 1951 or '52 using a 'KB' as my mark. While I worked for the White Hogan I stamped it with a small hogan." After leaving White Hogan, he incorporated more turquoise into his work, using only the highest-quality natural stones, and his designs kept a very modern feel.

1- *Naja* and collar handmade by Kenneth Begay (Navajo) while working at White Hogan. *Private collection.*

2- Handmade hinged bracelet by Kenneth Begay (Navajo), designed and made at White Hogan.

Mark Chee

(Navajo, 1914–1981)

Mark Chee was born at Lukachukai, Arizona, and educated in the Indian school system. By the age of twenty, he was working as a silversmith in Santa Fe for Julius Gans at Southwest Arts and Crafts. Chee enlisted in the Army in 1942 and served in the Air Force during the war; returning to Santa Fe in 1946, he married a woman from San Juan Pueblo where they made their home.

At this time, Chee was employed by Al Packard at Chaparral Trading Post in Santa Fe, and he worked in the shop for many years, likely until the early 1960s. He was recognized as one of the most skilled Navajo silversmiths working at that time. He won many awards for jewelry and especially for his sets of handmade silver flatware. A single table service required at least a month of work and was usually accomplished between the time he was making jewelry for orders or for sale in the shop.

1- Stamped cuff bracelet made by Mark Chee (Navajo). *Courtesy Karen Sires.*

2- Two bracelets and a ring made by Mark Chee (Navajo) with Number 8 turquoise settings. *Courtesy White collection.*

3- Pill boxes, thunderbird pin, and button, all marked with an arrowhead hallmark used by unknown silversmith, c. 1935.

It was reported in the *Santa Fe New Mexican* newspaper in 1958 that Chee made his own tools and only utilized the modern implements of torch, electric buffer, and silver saws. He worked in all techniques of silverwork including overlay, inlay, and hand-stamping, but is best known for his very heavy-gauge bracelets set with high-quality turquoise stones. His most recognized bracelets consist of either heavy solid bands with deep chisel work or split-shank cuffs with turquoise stones set between massive carinated bands. Chee signed his work using a right-facing thunderbird with his last name in the body of the bird. He worked into the late 1970s and passed away in August 1981 after a lengthy illness.

Willie Coin

(Hopi, 1904–1992)

Willie Coin dressed for a Hopi ceremony. *Courtesy Mary Coin Rogge.*

Willie Coin's family settled in Kykotsmovi after involvement in the 1906 disagreement that caused many families to leave Oraibi. In the fall of 1919, Coin left the mesas to attend Phoenix Indian School, but did not return to school after the 1927 term. That fall he went to join his uncle Earl Numkina in the Los Angeles area where they acted in the San Gabriel Mission Play, and Numkina taught his nephew silversmithing while they were in California.

Coin returned to Hopi during the Depression to settle in Bacavi. In 1947, he was hired as custodian at the Museum of Northern Arizona in Flagstaff where he lived on the grounds. Later he worked as an artist-in-residence demonstrating weaving, though he made silver occasionally, as well as carving kachinas and making moccasins. He retired from MNA in 1989 and moved back to Bacavi where he passed away in April 1992.

Most of Willie Coin's silverwork was done in the overlay style, but early unsigned work may have been more like Navajo-styled jewelry of the time. Shortly after he was employed by MNA in 1947, Coin began using a hallmark on his silver that was a gourd-shaped outline with three dots inside to signify the Hopi god Masau'u.

Overlay bolo tie made for Barton Wright by Willie Coin (Hopi). *Courtesy Barton Wright.*

Overlay ring by Willie Coin (Hopi). *Courtesy White collection.*

JOE H. QUINTANA

(Cochiti, 1915–1991)

Photo of Joe H. Quintana (Cochiti) soldering silver in 1951 at Turquoise Post in Los Alamos, New Mexico.

Jose Higineo Quintana was born to Cipriano and Rosarita Quintana at Cochiti Pueblo. At some point, he Americanized his name and became known as Joe H. Quintana. He would say later in life that it was about 1932 when he started working silver, adapting his blacksmithing and welding skills to this new medium.

By 1938, Quintana was employed by Julius Gans at Southwest Arts and Crafts in Santa Fe as one of five Cochiti silversmiths who worked for Gans on a piecework basis. John Adair noted in his book that Quintana was one of the most successful of these silversmiths, earning $1,000 a year around 1940.

Gans initiated the piecework system around 1938; he supplied silver slugs to some smiths who would make items in their home on their own schedule. These items were marked with an "S" hallmark to indicate they were made from slug silver. Quintana said, in 1983, that he "hammered and hammered, stamped and filed and polished. Always by hand." When he had quite a few finished pieces, he would walk fifteen miles from Cochiti to the highway where he would catch a bus to Santa Fe to deliver them to Gans for payment.

In the early 1940s, Quintana married Terecita Chalan, also of Cochiti, and they had five children, one of whom, Cipriano, would eventually change his name to Cippy CrazyHorse and continue his father's jewelry-making traditions. Terecita participated in Joe's silverwork by helping with his unique designs.

During World War II, it has been said, Quintana utilized his welding skills working in Navy shipyards in California. By 1951, he was back in New Mexico working for a time at the Turquoise Post in Los Alamos. In 1959, Quintana was employed as a silversmith and a designer at Seligman's in Albuquerque. During his career, he also worked at the Covered Wagon in Albuquerque and Packard's in Santa Fe. In the mid-1960s, Quintana was awarded a combined total of twenty-two ribbons from the Gallup Inter-Tribal Ceremonial and the New Mexico State Fair.

In 1966, Quintana began working in the shop at Irma's Indian Arts and Pawn in Albuquerque. One of his traditional concho belts from this time was purchased by Jim Morrison of The Doors and has been immortalized in vintage photographs of Morrison at the height of his career. Irma's closed in late 1971, and Joe returned to Cochiti where he continued to make jewelry and operated a curio shop and general store in the village.

Matching pins by Joe H. Quintana (Cochiti). *Courtesy Karen Sires.*

Quintana was interviewed in August 1983 by the *Santa Fe Reporter* for the upcoming Indian Market at which he would exhibit. He confided that some of his pieces of jewelry sold for well over the $1,000 he once made as an annual salary from silversmithing. He also said that he was making less jewelry than previously, but still had customers waiting for his completed work. He exhibited at Indian Market every year, but he did not enter any of the competitions any longer since awards "are for my son now. He is the tops. He is CrazyHorse."

Joe Quintana died December 19, 1991, in Cochiti and worked up until his death. In 2004, a major exhibit of his work, entitled "Joe H. Quintana: Master in Metal, Selections from the Irma Bailey Collection," opened at the Museum of Indian Arts and Culture in Santa Fe. Quintana most often signed his work JHQ, sometimes embellishing his hallmark with favorite stamps depicting pueblo clouds or lightning. Before the mid-1960s, he often added COCHITI below his hallmark stamp.

Bracelet with three turquoise settings by Joe H. Quintana (Cochiti). *Courtesy Karen Sires.*

Bolo tie, two bracelets, buckle, and pin by Joe H. Quintana (Cochiti). Concho bracelet approximately 3" long. According to his son, Cippy CrazyHorse, most pieces were made in the late 1950s, except for the spider pin which was made later.

Earrings by Joe H. Quintana. Left pair marked "JHQ;" right pair marked "Joe H. Quintana Cochiti NM." *Courtesy Karen Sires.*

Modern-design concho belt by Joe H. Quintana (Cochiti). *Courtesy White collection.*

Sam Roanhorse

(Navajo, 1916–1983)

The younger brother of Ambrose Roanhorse, Sam was born at Cornfields, Arizona. He attended the silversmithing class taught by his brother at the Santa Fe Indian School during the 1935–1936 terms. In 1940, he was employed as a silversmith at Southwest Arts and Crafts in Santa Fe; then he enlisted in the Army and served in the Navajo Signal Corps during World War II.

In 1949, Roanhorse worked for Fred Wilson's Indian Trading Post in Phoenix, and, in 1950, lived in Tucson for a few years working at various shops including Miller's Curios and Clay Lockett's. Later, he went to Scottsdale to work at the White Hogan. Sam Roanhorse passed away in March 1983.

Sam Roanhorse's hand-wrought jewelry is of the highest quality and displays the simple bold designs that his brother, Ambrose, advocated. He did not always sign his work, but his personal hallmark was SR, and, while working at the White Hogan, also included that shop stamp. Sometimes, he also hand-etched his name as a hallmark.

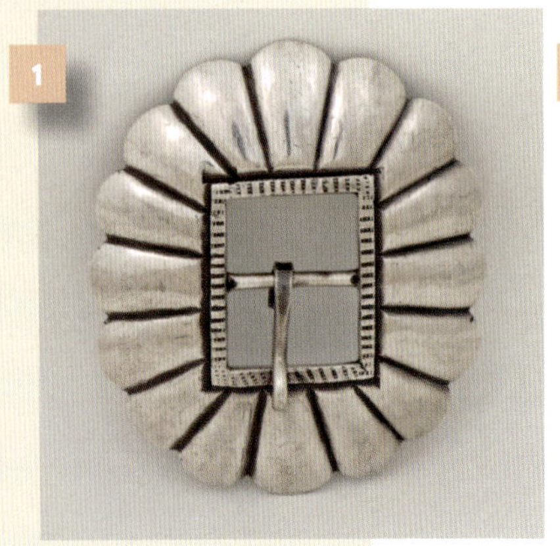

1- Unmarked buckle by Sam Roanhorse (Navajo), made while working for Clay Lockett in Tucson, 1950s.

2- Plain silver bracelet by Sam Roanhorse (Navajo), younger brother of Ambrose Roanhorse. *Courtesy Karen Sires.*

AMBROSE LINCOLN

(NAVAJO, 1917–1989)

For decades Ambrose Lincoln and Ambrose Roanhorse have unfortunately been described as being the same person, when in fact, they were distinctly different individuals. Much of Lincoln's work has been erroneously attributed to Roanhorse. Although both were Navajo silversmiths, Lincoln was about eleven years younger than Roanhorse and did not distinguish himself as a silversmith the way Roanhorse did.

Lincoln attended Fort Wingate Indian School and graduated in 1939. John Adair in his book *Navajo and Pueblo Silversmiths* lists both Ambrose Lincoln and Ambrose Roanhorse on the same page of his appendix of Navajo silversmiths. Also, Jonathan Batkin notes that Adair's field notes of 1940 identify Lincoln then working at Zuni for both C. G. Wallace and Charles Kelsey. Ironically, Lincoln worked as the silversmithing instructor at Santa Fe Indian School in 1942, the same school where Roanhorse taught from 1931 to 1939.

Ambrose Lincoln most commonly produced cast silver pieces sometimes with turquoise channel inlay, but it is uncertain if he did the inlay himself. At the Gallup Inter-Tribal Ceremonial of 1956, he collaborated with Lambert Homer (Zuni) to win the Second Place Grand Prize for a channel-work bracelet.

Ambrose Lincoln served in the Army during World War II. He died in 1989 and is buried in Gallup. Lincoln's work is signed with a capital "A" inside a keystone-shaped design.

Rainbow Yei necklace inlaid with turquoise by Ambrose Lincoln (Navajo), signed with a capital "A" in a keystone. *Courtesy Karen Sires.*

ALLEN POOYOUMA

(HOPI, 1922–2014)

From Hotevilla, Allen Pooyouma learned silversmithing at age fifteen from his father Gene Nuvhoyouma and uncle Ralph Tawangyawma. He used traditional hammer-and-file techniques at first.

Because of a bad eye, Pooyouma was ineligible to serve in World War II, so he started working as a commercial silversmith off the reservation for Doc Williams Saddle and Curio Shop in Flagstaff. He worked there for about three years, mainly setting petrified wood in rings. About 1946, Pooyouma moved back to Hotevilla.

In 1947, Ralph Tawangyawma was working at the Santa Rita Indian Shop, and he suggested that Pooyouma move to Tucson and join him in the shop, where they worked together for many years. Pooyouma stayed busy making special orders, but if there were not any, he was able to make his own designs.

Domed, hollow corn pin made by Allen Pooyouma (Hopi).

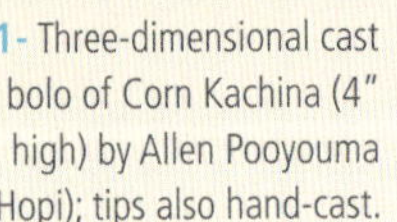

1- Three-dimensional cast bolo of Corn Kachina (4" high) by Allen Pooyouma (Hopi); tips also hand-cast.

2- Pieces utilizing various silver techniques—overlay earrings, appliqué buckle, cast pin, and hand-fabricated roadrunner pin—by Allen Pooyouma (Hopi).

3- Bracelet and ring by Allen Pooyouma (Hopi), employing designs similar to those used at the Thunderbird Shop.

4

5

4- Four bolo ties made by Allen Pooyouma (Hopi). The bird designs used on the right and left bolos were Pooyouma's favored designs.

5- Modern-design necklace and earring set by Allen Pooyouma (Hopi), utilizing design made popular by the Thunderbird Shop.

Pooyouma's standard techniques were stamp work and overlay; his most frequently used design was a stylistic overlay parrot with long tail feathers. He left Tucson about 1970, moving to Holbrook where his wife began teaching school.

Allen Pooyouma started using a hallmark of an ear of corn possibly from 1938 to 1940, and he used two variations of that hallmark: one with cross-hatching and one with dots.

6- Teaspoons made by Frank Vacit (Zuni). Vacit used his corn or fleur-de-lis hallmark as a design element in the bowls and along the handles of each spoon. Vacit not only made silver for C. G. Wallace, but also for Kelsey Trading Company of Zuni.

7- Four bracelets made by Fred Thompson (Navajo, 1922–2002). Right bracelet has Thompson's hallmark stamped on exterior of terminals; other bracelets are marked on interior. Thompson worked for Turpen Trading Post in Gallup in the 1950s. *Courtesy White collection.*

6

7

8- Bracelet, earrings, and watch bracelet made by Johnnie Mike Begay (Navajo). This design is considered to have been Begay's original design and often termed "railroad tracks." Johnnie Mike was the brother of Kenneth Begay.

9- Split-shank bracelet by Johnnie Mike Begay (Navajo) patterned after a White Hogan design. Though Begay worked at the White Hogan for an undetermined period, this piece is marked only with his JMB hallmark.

1- Double-row bracelet with turquoise disk beads plus coral and jet inlays by Charles Loloma (Hopi), purchased from the artist in 1963 at Bahti Indian Arts in Tucson.

2- Earrings and cast buckle, both unmarked, early 1960s by Charles Loloma (Hopi).

3- Cast *naja* by Charles Loloma (Hopi). *Private collection.*

4- Tufa-cast bracelet with multistone inlay on interior, made by Charles Loloma (Hopi). *Courtesy Karen Sires.*

CHARLES LOLOMA

(HOPI, 1921–1991)

No other Indian jeweler has received more accolades, or had more media exposure, than Charles Loloma. An internationally known artist, Loloma's greatest legacy is not just the masterful works of art he created, but also the horizons he opened for American Indian artists of all mediums.

Born at Hotevilla, Charles Loloma attended the village day school. Enrolling in Hopi High School in the fall of 1937, he studied art under Fred Kabotie, but transferred to Phoenix Indian School for his junior and senior years. Even as a student, his talent was recognized early and he quickly came to prominence as a muralist and painter.

Loloma entered the Army in 1942 and was discharged in 1946; afterwards he utilized the G.I. Bill to study ceramics in New York. It was during this time that he started dabbling in metalware and drew jewelry designs in a sketchbook; he would later state that he began making jewelry in 1947.

In 1954, Loloma moved to Scottsdale and opened a shop selling a line of fine art pottery; he then became increasingly interested in making jewelry. Although he picked up the basics of silversmithing on his own, he also observed the modern jeweler H. Fred Skaggs from whom he learned many advanced techniques. By 1956, publicity photos of his jewelry show Loloma working mainly in tufa casting, and his early silver creations exhibited designs that became the foundations of his career. During this time Loloma started gaining national recognition.

A few years later, Loloma was setting small pieces of turquoise and coral into his silver jewelry, and, in 1959, he demonstrated pottery and jewelry at the first Heard Museum Guild Indian Fair and Market. In the summer of 1960, Loloma taught silversmithing through the Southwestern Indian Art Project at the University of Arizona; the program lasted for three summers. Loloma also exhibited at Bahti Indian Arts in Tucson in 1963 and again in 1967.

In 1962, Loloma was hired as one of the teachers for the inaugural term of the Institute of American Indian Arts (IAIA) in Santa Fe, and the next year he made a trip to Paris where his jewelry was modeled in fashion previews. This impelled Loloma to work on his own, and, in 1965, he resigned from IAIA and returned to Hopi to build a home and studio in Hotevilla.

During the late 1960s, Loloma's reputation as a jeweler exploded. He won many First Place awards at Indian art shows, and his name became known outside of Indian art circles. In December 1971, Loloma was offered an important solo exhibition at the Heard Museum, the first recognition of his innovative jewelry design by a major institution.

By this time, Loloma could not meet the demands for his jewelry single-handedly, so he trained apprentices to assist with his orders in his Hotevilla studio. Eveli Sabatie worked from 1968 to 1972; his niece Verma Nequatewa began working in 1969, and her sister Sherian Honhongva followed in 1978.

The early 1970s was a time of great interest in Indian arts in general, and Indian jewelry in particular. Loloma had become quite successful, his fame expanded beyond the realm of Indian art, and he became internationally known. Loloma was involved in a tragic accident outside Hotevilla in September 1986 that left him unable to work. The studio closed in 1988, and Nequatewa and Honhongva started a line of their own jewelry designs marketed together under the name Sonwai. Today they work independently, each creating beautiful jewelry, and only Nequatewa uses the name Sonwai.

Loloma passed away on June 9, 1991; he will be remembered as an artist who broke away from the constraints of "traditional Indian art" and helped open new markets for the next generation of American Indian artists.

Charles Loloma signed his jewelry with a stylized version of his last name, sometimes carving it into the tufa mold, sometimes engraving it into the back of the piece or using a special chiseling tool.

1

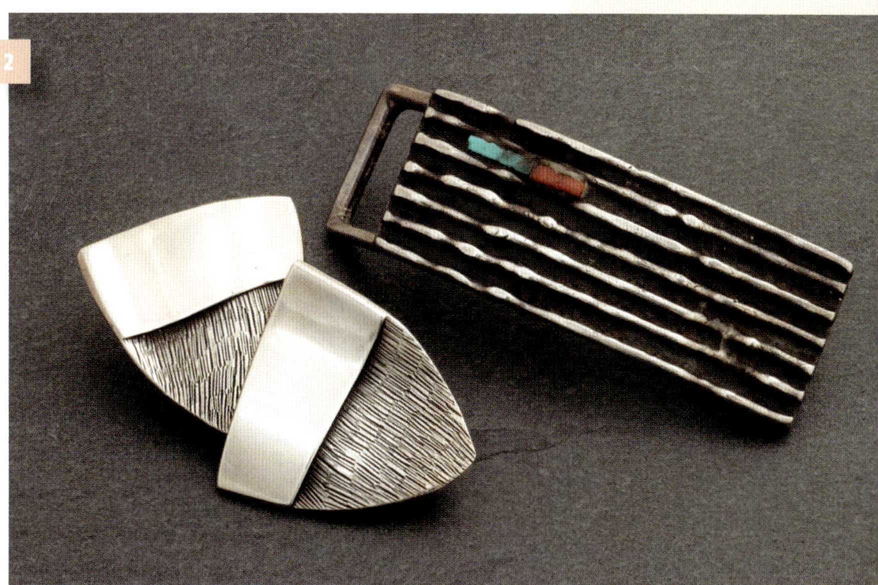
2

3

4

HARRY SAKYESVA

(Hopi, 1922–1969)

Harry Sakyesva was born at Hotevilla and graduated from Santa Fe Indian School before 1941. He received treatment in an Albuquerque sanatorium for a lung ailment between 1941 and 1945, and then moved to Santa Fe where he painted depictions of Hopi life for various galleries. Sakyesva was employed by the Thunderbird Shop as a silversmith in the early 1950s. His summers were spent working in the Santa Fe shop, while winters were spent in the Tucson shop. Frank Patania Jr. remembers Sakyesva worked for them for five or six years and during that time was in treatment periodically at the Indian Hospital.

Sometime before 1959, Sakyesva relocated to the Phoenix area. Because he worked in the overlay style, Emory and Wayne Sekaquaptewa hired him as a teacher for a silver business they planned to open. Sakyesva remained in Phoenix when the Sekaquaptewas relocated their Hopicrafts operation to Third Mesa.

In October 1961, Sakyesva Jewelry opened in Scottsdale, with Harry and Morris Robinson as the two Hopi craftsmen creating "fine custom made Hopi overlay" jewelry. But in August 1963, Sakyesva was a patient at National Jewish Hospital in Denver, and he remained there until sometime in 1964. One of Sakyesva's nurses remembers him well as a gentle-mannered and soft-spoken person, who clearly missed the Hopi mesas and longed for the day he would be well enough to return home. Sakyesva died in Scottsdale on October 22, 1969. His obituary reported that he had been a silversmith in the city for the last fifteen years.

Harry Sakyesva worked mainly in silver overlay, but sometimes utilized gold as accents and often incorporated turquoise settings. His work is signed with two tadpoles and SAKYESVA.

1-Silver bracelet set with turquoise by Harry Sakyesva (Hopi).

2- Three bolo ties by Harry Sakyesva (Hopi). Left has gold accents, bezel, and tips. Middle bolo is logo for Falstaff Beer.

Victor Coochwytewa

(Hopi, 1922–2011)

Raised at Shungopavi, Victor Coochwytewa learned silversmithing from Paul Saufkie, and, in 1941, was working for the Fred Harvey Company in Winslow. He served in the Army during World War II, and upon discharge in 1946, he attended leatherworking and silversmithing classes at Fort Wingate Indian School. He soon enrolled in the Hopi veterans' silversmithing classes taught at Oraibi, and, after the Hopi Silvercraft Guild was formed, Coochwytewa became a member.

By the mid-1950s, Coochwytewa had adapted leatherworking techniques to add a textured pattern to the background of his designs, thus creating what has become a standard design technique for Hopi overlay.

Coochwytewa continued to integrate new techniques in his jewelry, using turquoise and coral in the 1950s and 1960s. In the 1970s, he studied under Scottsdale designer Pierre Touraine, eventually incorporating gold and diamonds into his overlay jewelry. Throughout his career, he won top honors and, in 1994, was presented with the Arizona Indian Living Treasure Award. Coochwytewa passed away in 2011.

1

2

1- Concho belt, c. 1950–1955, made by Victor Coochwytewa (Hopi) while working at Hopi Silvercraft Guild; figures from Fred Kabotie's *Designs from the Ancient Mimbreños: With a Hopi Interpretation*. *Private collection.*

2- Early overlay bracelet, 1950s, made by Victor Coochwytewa (Hopi) while he was working at Hopi Silvercraft Guild. The raincloud hallmark is handmade from straight and circular design stamps. *Courtesy Karen Sires.*

3- Two bolo ties and necklace, 1950s, made by Victor Coochwytewa (Hopi). Hopi bird design necklace was advertised for $19 in the Hopi Silvercraft Guild mimeographed catalog.

4- Silver bolo tie with large turquoise setting by Victor Coochwytewa (Hopi), includes Hopi Silvercraft Guild trademark.

5- Palhik Mana belt buckle by Victor Coochwytewa (Hopi). Signed with raincloud hallmark and two Kopavi International shop marks, Kokopelli and liberty bell; the bell was used on pieces made in 1976. *Courtesy Robert F. Farling.*

It is unlikely that Victor Coochwytewa signed his pieces before he was involved in the veterans' classes. The earliest known hallmark, probably dating from 1950, was of a hand-formed raincloud, often included with a Hopi Guild Sunface stamp. Sometime later, probably in the 1960s, he made a single stamp for his hallmark that was a wide and narrow cloud with five lines of rain. On rare occasions, he added his initials VC to these marks. From 1976 until his retirement in 2006, Coochwytewa was represented by Kopavi Gallery in Sedona and would include the shop mark of a flute player on his pieces. He added a copyright mark around 1979.

JULiAN LOVATO

(Kewa, 1925–)

Julian Lovato's family were jewelry makers and, as a child, he observed his father and grandfather make silver and turquoise jewelry. He started making jewelry on his own in his teens and, when his father passed away just before 1940, may have worked for a short time at Maisel's in Albuquerque. Lovato enlisted in the Army in 1944, and upon returning to New Mexico in 1946, he married Marie Oyengue of San Juan Pueblo.

The following year, the Lovatos were living in Santa Fe and he was working as a silversmith at the Peasant Shop. During this time he worked in traditional jewelry designs. It was in 1952 that Frank Patania Sr. hired him to work in the Thunderbird Shop. By working with Patania, Lovato was introduced to new techniques and modern jewelry designs that influenced his career. Lovato continued to work at the Thunderbird Shop until Patania's death in 1964. When Patania's widow Aurora closed the Santa Fe shop, she bestowed the shop hallmark die upon Lovato, who become known as the "keeper of the thunderbird."

Sometime thereafter Lovato was employed by Packard's Chaparral Trading Post in Santa Fe, but he eventually moved back to Kewa Pueblo and built a successful career. He developed a contemporary style utilizing clean, elegant lines with layering of materials that he referred to as "dimensional." He designed his pieces around the shape of the setting and was able to work the bezel in such a way that the settings appear to float above the surface of the piece. His wife, Marie, worked with him; Julian designed and fashioned the jewelry, but she would do some of the more intricate finishing of pieces. She was also well known for her dot-and-dash designed and fabricated chains. They have worked in both silver and gold during their careers.

Lovato has won many awards since he began exhibiting his work in the late 1970s. He was also honored with the SWAIA Lifetime Achievement Award in 2002. Sadly, in March 2003, the family home in Kewa Pueblo was destroyed by fire. It is reported that Lovato has returned to making a small amount of jewelry when his health permits.

Julian Lovato signs his work J.LOVATO, STERLING, IHM (for Indian Hand Made) and included the thunderbird mark. When he worked for Packard's his pieces were signed J.LOVATO, STERLING, and included a PACKARDS shop mark.

1- Buckle, monogrammed letter opener, and 14-karat gold and coral ring by Julian Lovato (Kewa Pueblo).

2- Bolo made by Julian Lovato (Kewa Pueblo), while working at Packard's in Santa Fe, late 1960s.

PRESTON MONONGYE

(Mission/Mexican, 1927–1987)

Born in Los Angeles to a father of Mexican descent and a mother from a California Mission Indian tribe, Preston Monongye, at age seven, was taken to Hopi where he was adopted by David Monongye of the village of Hotevilla. He attended reservation schools including Hopi High School and, by the age of nine, Monongye was learning silversmithing from one of his Hopi uncles, Gene Pooyouma. He started by operating the bellows and later hammering silver into small bracelets.

Monongye served with the Army during World War II and reenlisted to serve in Korea for two years. He attended Haskell Institute and also took law courses in Los Angeles, eventually working for the Bureau of Indian Affairs in law enforcement on various southwest Indian reservations.

Early in the 1960s, Monongye decided to pursue silversmithing full-time and to concentrate on the overlay style then prevalent at Hopi. He transitioned from overlay to tufa casting and, in 1967, was employed by Tanner's Indian Arts and Crafts Center in Gallup. There he worked with inlay masters Eddie Beyuka (Zuni) and Lee and Mary Yazzie (Navajo). In the late 1960s and early 1970s, Monongye won many top prizes at Gallup Inter-Tribal Ceremonial and the New Mexico State Fair.

Moving from Gallup to Phoenix in 1972, Monongye continued to win awards at competitions across the Southwest throughout the 1970s. His work began to fetch top dollar, and he traveled and exhibited his jewelry as far away as Brussels and Paris. Though he was capable of inlay, in the early 1970s Monongye incorporated stones cut by Lee and Mary Yazzie and Lambert Homer Jr. (Zuni) into his jewelry.

Monongye died July 14, 1987. Though he is best known for his jewelry, he was a self-taught artist who also worked as a kachina carver, a painter, and a sculptor. In the early 1970s, he made a series of unique zinc plate etchings, some of which incorporated turquoise inlays.

Preston Monongye's overlay jewelry was typically signed with a "P" bordered underneath by a curved sawtooth design, sometimes including an angled sawtooth stamp on top. His early tufa-cast work was signed with only a capital "P;" but most of his tufa work was signed with a peyote bird with a capital "P" in the body.

1- Overlay pin and bracelet with Koyemsi (Mudhead) figures and buckle with deer design by Preston Monongye (Mission/Mexican), early 1960s.

2- Tufa-cast and inlay bolo tie and buckle by Preston Monongye (Mission/Mexican). Bolo marked with peyote bird hallmark, buckle with capital "P" mark.

3- Lidded silver overlay vessel, early 1970s, by Preston Monongye (Mission/Mexican) includes Mimbres designs and inlaid stones, marked with peyote bird hallmark. *Courtesy Heard Museum, Phoenix, Arizona, catalog # 4260-4a,b. Photograph by Craig Smith.*

4- Tufa-cast bracelet and two pendants by Preston Monongye (Mission/Mexican). *Courtesy White collection.*

LAWRENCE SAUFKIE | GRISELDA SAUFKIE

(Hopi, 1934–2011) | (Hopi, 1935–)

Lawrence Saufkie (Hopi), at the Heard Museum Guild Indian Fair and Market, March 2010.

Lawrence Saufkie was born at the Grand Canyon while his father, Paul Saufkie, worked there for the Fred Harvey Company. By the time Lawrence was thirteen, his father started teaching him the basics of silversmithing. Stamped copper buttons were some of his first products. Within the next year or two, Saufkie was selling overlay jewelry of his own creation at Gallup Inter-Tribal Ceremonial and, by age twenty, he would have his own booth. Once he married in 1953, Saufkie turned to silverwork as a full-time occupation. He then joined the Hopi Silvercraft Cooperative Guild and started using his hallmark of a bear shortly thereafter. He left the guild a few years later, stating, in 1975, that he preferred to work for himself with the ability to sell his jewelry where he chose.

Saufkie started winning awards as early as 1958. He exhibited at his first Indian Market in 1962, and his reputation grew as he began winning top honors at southwest shows in the late 1960s and early 1970s. By 1975 he was having difficulty keeping up with the demand for his work.

Jewelry made by Lawrence Saufkie (Hopi). Bolo tie 1957, bracelet 1963, rattle pendant and matching earrings 1960s, buttons 1990s. Bolo and bracelet marked only with bear hallmark, buttons marked with bear variation and SAUFKIE, rattle pieces unmarked.

Koyemsi (Mudhead) and Avanyu (Water Serpent) design bracelet, pendant with lapis lazuli setting, both by Lawrence Saufkie (Hopi). *Courtesy White collection.*

Griselda Nuvamsa, who grew up in Shungopavi, is a traditional basket weaver. Ten years after her marriage to Lawrence Saufkie in 1953, she used his tools to teach herself silversmithing; Griselda has been credited as the first woman to make silver at Hopi. By 1965, she began using her own hallmark and exhibited at shows alongside Lawrence, winning awards for both silverwork and basketry.

Their creative work of four decades was recognized in 1998, when Lawrence and Griselda Saufkie were both recipients of the Arizona Indian Living Treasure Award, the first married couple to be given that honor. Lawrence was also bestowed with a SWAIA Lifetime Achievement Award in 2007. He passed away June 14, 2011.

Lawrence's work was always of the highest quality and typically all silver overlay with traditional Hopi elements. Griselda would help with the creation of certain designs. Beginning in the early 1950s, Lawrence used a small silhouette of a bear as his hallmark because he was born into the Bear Clan. Later, he would add his last name and STERLING stamps to his mark. Griselda began marking her work in 1965 with an elongated raincloud, but that stamp broke; since 1972, she used a squared-off squatty cloud mark.

Silver bolo tie with roadrunner design, c. 1965–1971, made by Griselda Saufkie (Hopi).

BERNARD DAWAHOYA

(Hopi, 1936–2010)

Bernard Dawahoya was a very traditional Hopi man as well as a prolific and influential silversmith. As a religious leader of Shungopavi, he gave much of his time and effort to the village. He endeavored for Hopis to live as traditionally as possible. By teaching others how to work silver and providing an outlet for their finished goods, he hoped to enable them to live on the mesas and support their families. Many fine artists apprenticed at Dawahoya's workshop, among them his daughter Berna and her husband Anderson Koinva, who are working in the overlay style and continuing to use Bernard's designs.

Dawahoya was born at Shungopavi, and as a teen he spent much time herding sheep for his uncle Sidney Sekakuku Sr. who—along with clan relative Washington Talayumptewa—taught the art of silversmithing to young Bernard. He then worked for a short time with the Hopi Silvercraft Guild, possibly as early as 1956. Dawahoya was in Phoenix in 1960, helping Emory and Wayne Sekaquaptewa start a new jewelry business entitled Hopi Enterprises. Honing his skills with veteran silversmith Harry Sakyesva, who also worked for the Sekaquaptewas, he learned design techniques from another employee, artist Peter Shelton, who designed much of the new jewelry. In 1963, when the Sekaquaptewas relocated the business to Kykotsmovi on the Hopi reservation, Dawahoya moved back to his village. By the summer of 1966, he had left Hopicrafts and opened his own workshop and retail business, Dawa's Hopi Arts and Crafts, in Shungopavi. Over the years, he won many awards and honors, including being named an Arizona Indian Living Treasure in 1989.

In February 2010, Dawahoya passed away; he is considered one of the most prominent silversmiths of his generation. He used heavier gauge silver than most overlay artists, and his designs were bold and elegant; his cuts were crisp and precise. He mastered not only jewelry forms but also lidded boxes and seed pots. He used a few variations of the same snow cloud hallmark his whole career, with either three or four down-facing triangles; his early pieces also included the shop marks for the Hopi Silvercraft Guild or Hopicrafts.

Silver pot (3" dia.) with Horned Water Serpent design made by Bernard Dawahoya (Hopi). *Courtesy Robert F. Farling.*

Belt buckle by Bernard Dawahoya (Hopi). Two running quails was one of his most popular designs.

Jewelry made by Bernard Dawahoya (Hopi). Bolo tie inlaid with turquoise and coral was used as the prototype for six cast copies worn by members of the Phoenix City Council, early 1960s.

THE LOVATO FAMILY

(KEWA PUEBLO)

Santo Domingo Pueblo, which officially restored the traditional name of Kewa Pueblo in 2010, is a village known for its centuries-old jewelry tradition. The Lovato family, in particular, descended from Valentino Coriz, is renowned for their beautiful cast silver and mosaic inlay jewelry. Valentino, born about 1885, handmade turquoise beads that he often traded outside of the village.

Ring and pendant by Harold Lovato, cross by Leo Coriz, both from Kewa Pueblo. *Courtesy White collection.*

One of his sons, **Santiago Leo Coriz**, was born in 1913 and learned to make beads from his father. As a young man he also learned tufa casting from a Hopi friend, but when he first started making silver jewelry it was more traditionally fabricated. Coriz served in the Navy during World War II and, because he was categorized as a metalsmith, was put to work repairing bullet holes in airplanes. At the time of his death in 1997, Coriz was a spiritual leader of the pueblo and caretaker of one of the two kivas in the village; he was well respected and liked by everyone who encountered him. Coriz had a successful career as a silversmith and worked not only in tufa casting, but also in overlay with Pueblo designs as well as in the traditional Navajo style; his work is stamped LEO CORIZ.

One of the five children fathered by Coriz was daughter Mary, born into the Corn Clan in 1936, who says she was raised very traditionally. Instructed by her father and mother, **Mary Coriz Lovato** started working in shell at age eighteen but previously made thunderbird necklaces utilizing recycled plastic and phonograph records. After a visit to an Arizona museum, Mary was inspired by the mosaic work done on shell by the prehistoric Hohokam people, and, as a result, she revived traditional Pueblo shell inlay work in the late 1950s. Mary's designs were continuously evolving and, in the mid-1970s, she began incorporating silver into her mosaic work, affording it a more contemporary appearance and winning awards at many shows. While raising a family Mary never ceased making jewelry, especially earrings and pendants, seeing it as a way to help support her family. Her initials McL are usually etched onto the obverse of her work.

Mosaic inlay shell pendants, hand pendant, and earrings by Mary C. Lovato (Kewa Pueblo). Hallmark has been outlined for better visibility. Shell pendants, *courtesy Madeleine Nash.* Others, *authors' collection.*

Tufa-cast bracelets by Kewa Pueblo silversmiths. Upper by Sedelio Lovato. Lower bracelet unmarked by Sedelio's son, Harold Lovato.

In the early 1950s, Mary Coriz married **Sedelio Fidel Lovato**, also born at Santo Domingo in 1929. Sedelio learned the art of tufa casting from his father-in-law Leo Coriz and began working in the late 1950s. His silver incorporated channel and mosaic inlay turquoise with elegant traditional designs and won awards in the early 1970s. Sedelio has done little silverwork for the last few years. His work is marked with his initials SFL, which are usually carved into the tufa mold.

Brass concho belt, early 1970s, by Harold Lovato (Kewa Pueblo).

Of Mary and Sedelio's six sons, the most prominent jewelers are Harold and Anthony. Born in 1954, **Harold Lovato** learned tufa casting as a young man. He was winning awards at Indian Market and the Eight Northern Indian Pueblos show in the early 1970s. He made a practice of carving into both sides of the tufa mold, so designs appeared on every surface. He utilized a variety of gemstones for inlay work and would often set a single large turquoise stone in a unique pronged bezel. Harold Lovato passed away in 1997. He was an expert in tufa casting and innovator in design. His work is marked with a conjoined HL and sometimes includes a cornstalk.

Anthony Lovato was born in 1958. At fifteen years of age, he began making heshi beads and mosaic shell jewelry under his mother's guidance. He also learned tufa casting from his father and grandfather and was working in that style in 1975. He attended the Institute of American Indian Arts, majored in metals, and graduated in 1978 with a Fine Arts degree. The next year he took a job at Museum of Northern Arizona in Flagstaff and also took additional jewelry classes at Northern Arizona University. He would later attend jewelry classes at University of Colorado at Boulder. Returning to Kewa Pueblo in 1982, Anthony became a full-time jeweler two years later. Today, Lovato is a well-respected jeweler who works in silver and gold receiving awards at all the major Indian art shows in the country. As a member of the Corn Clan, much of his work depicts images of corn. Bold hand-fabricated link chains often complement his Corn Maiden figures, whose faces are represented by gemstones. Lovato credits Apache sculptor Allan Houser, Hopi jeweler Charles Loloma, and his grandfather Leo Coriz as his main influences. His work, which deftly incorporates traditional Pueblo imagery with contemporary design, is marked with a conjoined AL, either KEWA or previously SDP for Santo Domingo Pueblo, and the last two digits of the year of creation.

Tufa-cast corn bracelet and ring, Corn Maiden pendant, and handmade stamped chain, all by Anthony Lovato (Kewa Pueblo).

A fifth generation of the Coriz/Lovato family has already begun gaining attention. Anthony Lovato's sons, **Joel Pajarito** and **Cordell Pajarito**, are continuing the tufa-casting tradition begun by their great-grandfather Leo Coriz. Joel, born in 1984, and his younger brother Cordell, born 1988, each were awarded ribbons only two years after they began to work in silver. Their reputations have grown rapidly; in 2007, Cordell received the Tsepe' Award for Youth at the Eight Northern Indian Pueblos show, and, in 2008, Joel was the recipient of the Malcolm and Connie Goodman Fellowship for Emerging Native American Artists at the Wheelwright Museum. Their work continues to evolve as they find their personal approaches to traditional designs. They sign their work with their first names, either KEWA or SDP, and the last two digits of the year of creation.

The remarkable legacy of the Coriz and Lovato families—never copying from the previous generation but creating their own fresh and unique style—will no doubt continue with each generation and advance tufa casting into more modern realms.

1

2

1- Kewa Pueblo artists (left to right): Joel Pajarito, Cordell Pajarito, and their father, Anthony Lovato, at the Heard Museum Indian Fair and Market, March 2010.

2- Jewelry by Kewa Pueblo brothers Joel Pajarito and Cordell Pajarito. Left bracelet and pendant by Joel. Right bracelet and pendant by Cordell. *Courtesy David West/Gallery West.*

MICHAEL KABOTIE

(Hopi, 1942–2009)

Internationally renowned Hopi artist Michael Kabotie was born to Fred and Alice Kabotie at the Second Mesa village of Shungopavi. He grew up surrounded by his father's award-winning artwork. He attended reservation schools before enrolling in the University of Arizona to study engineering, but never completed the courses. While his father was director of the Hopi Silvercraft Cooperative Guild, Michael became acquainted with the silversmiths working there. In 1958, Wallie Sekayumptewa instructed Kabotie in the overlay technique, and Michael's cousins Walter Polelonema, McBride Lomayestewa, and Mark Lomayestewa were also influential in his development as a silversmith. During the 1960s, Kabotie immersed himself in painting and put silverwork aside.

Kabotie left the mesas and attended Haskell Institute, graduating in 1961. Returning to Hopi, he was initiated into the Wuwutsim Society in 1967 and given the Hopi name Lomawywesa (Walking in Harmony). While establishing his reputation as an acclaimed painter, Kabotie nonetheless returned to silversmithing in the late 1970s.

Not only was he innovative as a painter, but also as a silversmith. Building upon the overlay technique by using contemporary construction methods bestowed a sense of depth to his work. His designs echoed those from his paintings; they were steeped in Hopi culture, most notably from the murals at Awatobi and pottery from the village of Sikyatki. He worked independently and traveled often to exhibit at fairs and shows, including Indian Market from 1982 to 1999, as well as lecturing and consulting for museum exhibitions. Though Kabotie is best known as an artist, he considered jewelry to be his livelihood, stating to CNN correspondent Bill Tucker in 2000, "Jewelry is my job. Art and painting is my journey."

In 2003, Kabotie was selected as a recipient of the Arizona Indian Living Treasure Award, and, in 2006, he was awarded a fellowship from the National Museum of the American Indian.

Kabotie and son Paul Kabotie posted on the Native Art Network website concerning hallmarks attributed to his silverwork. Michael confirmed that while experimenting with silversmithing in the mid-1960s, he made a few pieces of traditional overlay that are hallmarked with a letter "K" adapted from his father's hallmark stamp. These pieces would not have stone settings and would be extremely rare. When Kabotie began to make jewelry professionally in the late 1970s, he used his signature of *Lomawywesa* as a hallmark on his pieces, which is the only hallmark he would ever use. Most of Kabotie's work is made from silver, though some pieces incorporate gold highlights and others are made entirely of gold; he seldom used gemstone settings.

Michael Kabotie died from complications of the H1N1 (swine flu) virus on October 23, 2009.

Bolo tie by Michael Kabotie (Hopi), signed "Lomawywesa, © 83".

Bracelet and necklace with abstract Hopi designs by Michael Kabotie (Hopi). *Courtesy Doris Roland.*

Bolo tie, hair barrette, collar, pendant, and bracelet made of silver and gold by Michael Kabotie (Hopi). *Courtesy White collection.*

Cippy CrazyHorse

(Cochiti, 1946–)

Cippy CrazyHorse, like his father Joe H. Quintana, excels in making jewelry utilizing simple but elegant designs. Born at Cochiti Pueblo as Cipriano Quintana, he was not initially interested in becoming a silversmith. After graduating from high school, he attended Eastern New Mexico University where he majored in anthropology.

Afterward he joined the Navy, where he served in a submarine fleet and met his wife, Sue, while stationed in Connecticut; they were married in 1971. Returning to Cochiti after his stint in the service, he took a job with a construction company building Cochiti Dam. But, in 1974, a work accident left CrazyHorse disabled and unable to continue a career in construction. It was then that he began to turn to silversmithing in order to support his family. The change in careers resulted in a change of his last name, from Quintana to CrazyHorse.

Cippy CrazyHorse (Cochiti) wearing one of his handmade squash blossom necklaces at the Heard Museum Guild Indian Fair and Market, March 2011.

CrazyHorse is mostly self-taught, though he had absorbed knowledge of silversmithing from living in a home of artists. As quoted in Kari Chalker's *Totems to Turquoise*,

> My mother's advice came back to me. She used to say, "Go watch your father do silverwork, for some day that may help you." I'm glad I did that because my parents were both good teachers; they were a good team and made beautiful jewelry.

His parents encouraged his efforts and after a few years CrazyHorse realized he had inherited his father's ability to work silver and his mother's design skills. This set him on a path to a successful career. From the beginning he worked in the old way, which is more time intensive, but he believes it produces better results. Rarely using sheet silver, he prefers to melt silver into ingots that he rolls by hand or hammers into shape.

One of his first major awards was in 1978 at Santa Fe Indian Market where he won the School of American Research Prize for Excellence in Traditional Design in Jewelry for a two-strand bead necklace designed by his mother. Not surprisingly, his father had won the exact same award in 1970 for an all-silver concho belt.

In addition to hand fabrication, he utilizes tufa-casting techniques, and his designs are created with chisels or stamps, or by repoussé. CrazyHorse initially signed his work with CZH, but for many years has used a backwards "C" and a forward "C" joined in the back.

Like his father before him, he is active in the pueblo, serving as governor and lieutenant governor, and his family participates in village dances.

Bracelets, necklace, and ring by Cippy CrazyHorse (Cochiti). *Courtesy Jed Foutz, Shiprock Santa Fe.*

HOWARD SICE

(Hopi/Laguna,, 1948–)

Howard Sice (Hopi/Laguna), March 2010, at the Heard Museum Guild Indian Fair and Market.

Howard Sice is of Hopi and Laguna Pueblo heritage and was raised in the Laguna village of Paraje. During his youth he spent time with Hopi aunts on the mesas. Born in Winslow, Sice spent twenty years in the Air Force and is a veteran of the Vietnam War. He married Patricia Smith (Navajo) who is from a family of jewelers, and Sice learned the basics of silversmithing from her father in 1972. By 1981, he had developed his signature style of engraving designs on silver and gold, later adding exotic metals such as titanium to his repertoire. After leaving the military, Sice returned to Tucson—where he had been stationed for a time—and dedicated himself to becoming an artist. He is well known for beautifully crafted silver boxes and seed pots.

Sice won his first competitive award in 1982 and has since won many others including Best of Show at Museum of Northern Arizona's Hopi Exhibition, First Place at the Heard Museum Guild Indian Fair and Market, and a SWAIA Fellowship in 1992. Besides jewelry, he has also worked as a designer of sculptures and furniture in various metals such as steel, copper, and bronze, and of roadway beautification projects in the Phoenix metropolitan area. Sice is constantly progressing in both design and materials and taking on new projects. He signs his work by stamping or hand-engraving SICE.

1

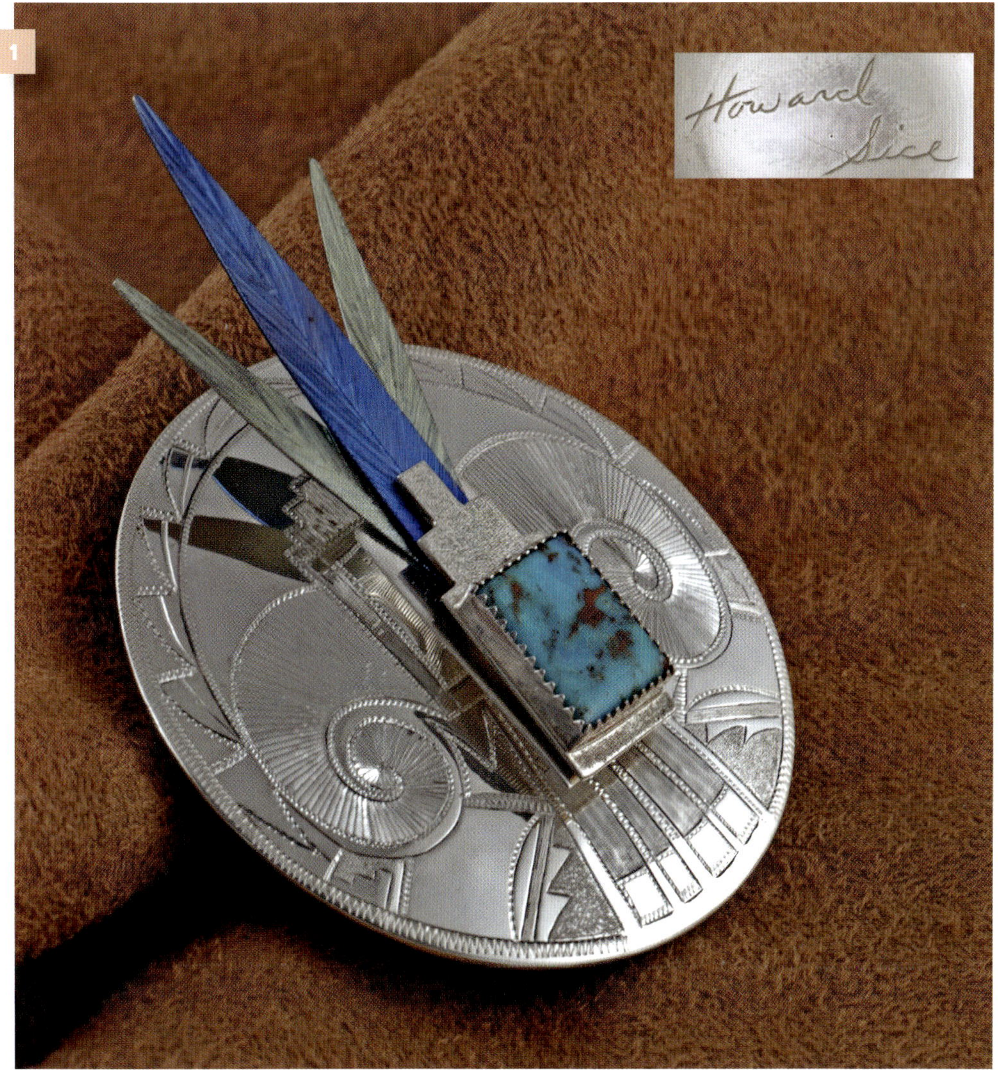

2

1- Lidded silver seed pot, 2007, by Howard Sice (Hopi/Laguna). Feathers on lid made from titanium; turquoise stone is from Pilot Mountain mine.

2- Etched bracelet made by Howard Sice (Hopi/Laguna).

3- Three silver seed pots, early 1990s, by Howard Sice (Hopi/Laguna).

4- Overlay ram buckle by Hyson Craig (Navajo); bolo tie and mixed-metal wedding basket pin by Willie Yazzie Sr. (Navajo).

5- Sterling and 14-karat gold necklace with multistone inlay by Roy Talahaftewa (Hopi). From Shongopavi, Talahaftewa attended the Institute of American Indian Arts in Santa Fe and has won many top honors. He frequently combines overlay and tufa-casting techniques. *Courtesy Doris Roland.*

EDISON CUMMINGS

(NAVAJO, 1962–)

Of all the younger generations of Navajo smiths who worked for White Hogan, none followed in Kenneth Begay's footsteps more than Edison Cummings, with his mastery of techniques and innovative designs.

Cummings, born at Keams Canyon, studied painting as a teen and attended the Institute of American Indian Arts where he graduated in 1984 with a degree in three-dimensional art. Afterward he became intrigued with metalwork while attending Arizona State University. Cummings started working at White Hogan in 1990 and learned to incorporate silver with ironwood and gradually progressed to creating his own designs. In 1996, he entered his first jewelry competition with a stunning teapot and won Best of Class and Best in Division at the Heard Museum Guild Indian Fair and Market. Cummings says he left White Hogan in 1996 to work on his own.

Cummings continues to win awards at shows across the Southwest for his fine vessels and jewelry. At the 2006 Indian Market, he won Best of Classification for a graceful coffee pot with an ironwood handle. Cummings is one of the most versatile silversmiths working at this time, producing a wide variety of styles, from traditional jewelry with stamped and repoussé designs, to modern tufa-cast bracelets and buckles, to fabricated purses, boxes, hollowware, and flatware. He works in both silver and gold, uses only high-quality stones including turquoise, coral, and gemstones, and still incorporates ironwood into many pieces. He is as comfortable doing paintings and sculpture as he is creating jewelry.

Cummings first hallmarked his jewelry with a buffalo skull that he used while riding bulls on the rodeo circuit. Beginning in 1996 and continuing to the present, he has used E.CUMMINGS as his identification stamp. Because of their design, many of his contemporary pieces are not able to be stamped with his hallmark.

1- Edison Cummings (Navajo), March 2010, at Heard Museum Guild Indian Fair and Market.

2- Silver bracelet set with ironwood marked with buffalo skull; silver and 14-karat gold bracelets and ring unmarked. All pieces by Edison Cummings (Navajo).

PERRY SHORTY

(NAVAJO, 1964–)

In the mid-1980s, Perry Shorty was in his early twenties and worked in a jewelry supply shop in Gallup. The silversmiths who were his customers talked to him about their silverworking experiences, which sparked an interest in Shorty to try his hand at the craft. He is a first-generation Navajo silversmith and credits Raymond Yazzie for teaching him to cut and to grind stones.

In 1990, Shorty quit his job and pursued jewelry full-time, entering the competition at the Gallup Inter-Tribal Ceremonial that year. Winning his first major award in 1994 at Ceremonial for cluster work, he also exhibited at Indian Market that same year. The next year he won a fellowship from SWAIA, while offering pieces made with hand-hammered ingot silver.

Shorty gained knowledge of the techniques of early Navajo silver by researching old jewelry in museums and private collections. Trying to keep the integrity of the old style, Shorty uses the same types of silver coins that early smiths would have used, minted from 1892 to 1916—well-worn coins termed "slickers" by coin collectors for their lack of detail—and melts them into ingots that are hand-hammered to create his First Phase style. Continuing in the tradition of the smiths he emulates, he uses as few tools as possible and also makes most of his own design stamps. Shorty prefers to use untreated, natural turquoise stones for his settings. He signs his work with *P. Shorty* and on items made from coins he also stamps *Coin Silver*.

1- Perry Shorty (Navajo) at the Heard Museum Guild Indian Fair and Market, March 2010.

2- Silver concho belt, bracelets, ring, squash blossom earrings, and oval tray by Perry Shorty (Navajo). The bracelets are also marked "Coin Silver."

3- Traditional-style silver bracelets with turquoise sets and earrings by Perry Shorty (Navajo). *Courtesy David West/Gallery West and White collection and authors' collection.*

LIZ WALLACE

(NAVAJO/WASHOE/MAIDU 1975–)

Liz Wallace was born in Northern California, and, although the daughter of notable jewelers, her current success is entirely of her own making. Her father made jewelry in the garage at home, but it was not until Liz took a metalsmithing class at Santa Fe Community College in 1996 that she learned to work silver. She stated that her first pieces were too contemporary and did not succeed. Turning to traditional Indian jewelry, she then designed a series of earrings that evoked old Navajo and Pueblo styles. These and her signature butterfly pins quickly brought her recognition. Once Wallace became familiar with lapidary skills, she began to cut her own stones using high-grade turquoise. The turquoise stones that are cut for earrings, butterflies, and dragonflies are typically cut in half horizontally and "book matched" for a mirrored effect.

1- Liz Wallace (Navajo/Washoe/Maidu) at the Heard Museum Guild Indian Fair and Market, March 2010.

2- Six insect pins by Liz Wallace (Navajo/Washoe/Maidu), two with wings made of enameled glass using the plique á jour technique. *Photo by Carolyn Wright, The Photography Studio. Courtesy Liz Wallace.*

In 2003, Wallace was invited to spend time with jeweler-historian Robert Bauver in his New Salem, Massachusetts, studio. He taught her a number of techniques, including plique á jour (a type of enamel) and how to raise silver to make hollowware. Raising is a difficult and time-consuming technique using a single flat piece of metal.

One of Wallace's most ambitious raised pieces is a vessel entitled "Suggestion of a Pond" for which she painstakingly hammered and shaped a six-inch diameter, eighteen-gauge sterling silver disk to form the body of the vessel. She estimated it took several thousand hammer strikes just to get it to its present shape. She then used a special hammer with a polished mirror-finish head to smooth out the surface; going over the entire surface with this small hammer six or more times to polish the body. Then she selected twenty turquoise stones from the Castle Dome mine, which she cut and polished to fit around the rim. Setting the bezels and stones took many days for a proper fit without any gaps. She explains, "I wanted to make a vessel that had turquoise around the rim, so that it was reminiscent of a pond with rocks around the edge. I also wanted to make the inside dark so that it was mysterious as well." "Suggestion of a Pond" took many hours of labor and skill and the result is a true work of art.

Wallace constantly expands her repertoire with diverse and innovative styles and techniques, from traditional to modern, making her one of today's most sought-after American Indian jewelers. Fascinated with the Art Nouveau style and greatly influenced by French jewelry and glass designer René Lalique, Wallace has incorporated design elements from these styles into her artwork. Among her many awards, Wallace won a fellowship from SWAIA in 2009 and has also garnered many First Place awards at Indian Market. In January 2011, a solo exhibit entitled "Nature Nutures: Jewelry by Liz Wallace" opened at the Wheelwright Museum of the American Indian in Santa Fe.

Though Wallace's earliest pieces were not signed, she tried out a few hallmarks before settling on the two most common versions. At first she used a vertical slash with a dot on either side that was usually scratched in shallow and faint but sometimes stamped. She also used her Chinese zodiac symbol of a rabbit on a few occasions. Then she used her initials LW conjoined at an offset with two dots above and below the "W." Most recently, she stamps or etches an "L" with two crossbars along the top in a design that resembles a dragonfly.

In an interesting twist of fate, the design stamps of Hopi silversmith Morris Robinson found their way into the talented hands of Ms. Wallace, who feels fortunate to extend the usefulness of a master silversmith's tools and believes Robinson would be pleased to know that his handmade stamps are still in use.

3- "Suggestion of a Pond" by Liz Wallace (Navajo/Washoe/Maidu), 2009. Raised from a 6" diameter silver disk with hand-selected matching Castle Dome turquoise sets around rim (4" dia.).

4- Jewelry by Liz Wallace (Navajo/Washoe/Maidu) including traditional-style earrings, orchid pins, stylized hearts, and blowfish and starfish from her ocean series. *Photo by Carolyn Wright, The Photography Studio. Courtesy Liz Wallace.*

KEE YAZZIE JR.

(NAVAJO, 1969–)

Kee Yazzie Jr. is a silversmith who has taken the technique of overlay to new heights. He grew up in Utah and studied architectural design in college. Yazzie is basically a self-taught artist from a family of silversmiths, but, in 1993, he apprenticed with Navajo jeweler Ray Scott and, by 1995, started working on his own. He also took workshops from Duane Maktima (Hopi/Laguna) in the late 1990s.

Gaining inspiration from work by silversmiths he admired, Yazzie quickly developed a style of his own and won his first award in 1995 at the Eight Northern Pueblos Arts and Crafts Show. His work is influenced not only by rock art he saw around his childhood home on the reservation, but also by patterns and designs from Navajo culture. Expert at many techniques, Yazzie incorporates overlay, appliqué, texturing, stamp work, gold accents, and a discreet use of stone settings in his ever-evolving designs. He continues to win awards and, in 2011, garnered the Best in Show at the Museum of Northern Arizona Navajo Market. Yazzie signs his jewelry with a stylized KEE.

Kee Yazzie Jr. (Navajo), March 2011, at the Heard Museum Guild Indian Fair and Market.

Chaco Canyon series bracelet (left top), overlay bracelet (right top), and appliqué double-headed Avanyu buckle (bottom), all by Kee Yazzie Jr. (Navajo).

VALUATION GUIDE

Hallmarked vintage or antique jewelry tends to demand higher prices than those pieces that are not marked by the maker. Many of the artists profiled in this volume are deceased, and even though they may have worked into the last few decades, their work tends to sell on the antique market. These artists are the most sought after by collectors of American Indian and modern jewelry, and the limited supply of their works will ensure that their value will continue to increase as new collectors enter the field.

Prices for named artists, especially those considered important in the development of Indian jewelry, can be unpredictable. Scarcity of pieces on the market would be the largest determinant of rising prices, but one highly motivated individual with unlimited resources can change the dynamics of the market in a very short time.

Most of these artists worked in many styles, which is one of the reasons their work is so sought after. But some styles are less desirable to the majority of collectors than others. For example, tufa-cast pieces by Preston Monongye will always command higher prices than the traditional Hopi overlay he made early in his career.

Traditionally, jewelry made to be worn by women (bracelets, necklaces, earrings) sell better than those made for men (buckles, bolos, cuff links), but because both sexes wear bracelets, they are always the most in demand and the highest priced. Some forms, such as squash blossom necklaces, concho belts, and bolos, tend to see more variance in their prices as fads and fashion styles come and go. Because of the relative scarcity and different audience for boxes, vessels, and flatware, their prices tend to stay higher than equivalent jewelry forms.

The volatility of the market makes it nearly impossible to predict or estimate prices for antique and vintage hallmarked jewelry. Unless a bargain can be found in secondhand stores or on the Internet, any bracelet hallmarked by a well-known artist will begin—as of early 2013—at approximately $400 and likely range well into the thousands of dollars. Boxes tend also to have a wide range of prices, from about $250 for a hallmarked pill box to more than $2,500 for ornate table boxes with settings. Exceptional items will always demand the highest price.

As long as antique Indian jewelry commands such high prices, there will always be counterfeits. Buyers should be aware that even fake jewelry made overseas and by Anglo silversmiths will often bear hallmarks. Genuine handmade Indian jewelry will often be expensive because they are unique, handcrafted, individually made creations. Mechanically produced or imported products from foreign labor will cost considerably less. Fakes and counterfeits are easily sold on the Internet where buyers cannot judge quality and workmanship. Even hallmarked pieces by well-known artists have been reproduced using lost-wax and spin-cast methods. The market for Charles Loloma's jewelry was nearly ruined a few years back when reproductions of his work appeared with forged hallmarks and sold for phenomenal prices. Many of these forgeries are still in private collections of unsuspecting buyers.

Awareness of the hallmarks, the styles the artists worked in, and experience in handling authentic antique jewelry will provide a solid basis for collectors.

Works by contemporary artists will vary in price based on name recognition and market demand. The rising cost of raw materials—silver, gold, and gemstones—also has a large bearing on the prices of contemporary jewelry.

SELECTED BIBLIOGRAPHY

Adair, John. *The Navajo and Pueblo Silversmiths*. Norman: University of Oklahoma Press, 1944.

Bahti, Mark. *Collecting Southwest Native American Jewelry.* New York: David McKay, 1980.

———. *Silver + Stone: Profiles of American Indian Jewelers.* Tucson: Rio Nuevo Press, 2007.

Batkin, Jonathan. *The Native American Curio Trade in New Mexico*. Santa Fe, NM: Wheelwright Museum of the American Indian, 2008.

Baxter, Paula A. *Southwest Silver Jewelry.* Atglen, PA: Schiffer, 2001.

Bedinger, Margery. *Indian Silver: Navajo and Pueblo Jewelers.* Albuquerque: University of New Mexico Press, 1973.

Bsumek, Erika Marie. *Indian-made: Navajo Culture in the Marketplace, 1868–1940*. Lawrence: University Press of Kansas, 2008.

Chalker, Kari, ed. *Totems to Turquoise: Native North American Jewelry Arts of the Northwest and Southwest.* New York: Harry N. Abrams, 2004.

Cirillo, Dexter. *Southwestern Indian Jewelry: Crafting New Traditions*. New York: Rizzoli International, 2008.

Kabotie, Fred. *Designs from the Ancient Mimbreños: With a Hopi Interpretation*. San Francisco, CA: Grabhorn Press, 1949.

———. *Hopi Silver.* Mimeographed catalog (November 1950). Oraibi, AZ: Hopi Silvercraft Guild.

Kabotie, Fred, and Bill Belknap. *Fred Kabotie: Hopi Indian Artist*. Flagstaff: Museum of Northern Arizona / Northland Press, 1977.

Lowry, Joe Dan, and Joe P. Lowry. *Turquoise: The World Story of a Fascinating Gemstone.* Layton, UT: Gibbs Smith, 2010.

McGibbeny, J. H. "Hopi Jewelry." *Arizona Highways*, July 1950.

Mangum, Richard, and Sherry Mangum. "The Hopi Silver Project of the Museum of Northern Arizona." *Plateau*, new series, no. 1 (1995).

Matthews, Washington. "Navajo Silversmiths." In *Second Annual Report to the Smithsonian Institute from the Bureau of Ethnology, 1880–1881.* Washington, DC: Government Printing Office, 1883.

Pardue, Diana F. "Native American Silversmiths in the Southwest." *American Indian Art Magazine* 30, no. 3 (Summer 2005).

———. *Contemporary Southwestern Jewelry.* Layton, UT: Gibbs Smith, 2007.

Rosnek, Carl, and Joseph Stacey. *Skystone and Silver: The Collector's Book of Southwest Indian Jewelry.* Englewood Cliffs, NJ: Prentice-Hall, 1976.

Schrader, Robert Fay. *The Indian Arts and Crafts Board: An Aspect of the New Deal Indian Policy.* Albuquerque: University of New Mexico Press, 1983.

Slaney, Deborah C. *Blue Gem, White Metal: Carvings and Jewelry from the C. G. Wallace Collection.* Phoenix, AZ: Heard Museum, 1998.

Trahant, LeNora Begay. *The Success of the Navajo Arts and Crafts Enterprise: A Retail Success Story.* New York: Walker, 1996.

U.S. Department of the Interior. Indian Arts and Crafts Board. *Reports and Documents Concerning the Activities of the Indian Arts and Crafts Board, December 1, 1943.* Washington, DC.

Van Ness Seymour, Tryntje. *When the Rainbow Touches Down.* Phoenix, AZ: Heard Museum, 1988.

Weigle, Marta, and Barbara A. Babcock, eds. *The Great Southwest of the Fred Harvey Company and the Santa Fe Railway.* Phoenix, AZ: Heard Museum, 1996.

Whiting, Arthur F. *Hopi Arts and Crafts Survey for the Indian Arts and Crafts Board*. 4 vols. 1942. No MS 108. Museum of Northern Arizona Archives, Flagstaff.

Woodward, Arthur. *Navajo Silver: A Brief History of Navajo Silversmithing.* Flagstaff, AZ: Northland Press, 1971.

Wright, Barton. *Hallmarks of the Southwest.* Rev. ed. Atglen, PA: Schiffer, 2000.

Wright, Margaret Nickelson. *Hopi Silver: The History and Hallmarks of Hopi Silversmithing.* 5th ed. Flagstaff, AZ: Northland Press, 1998.

INDEX

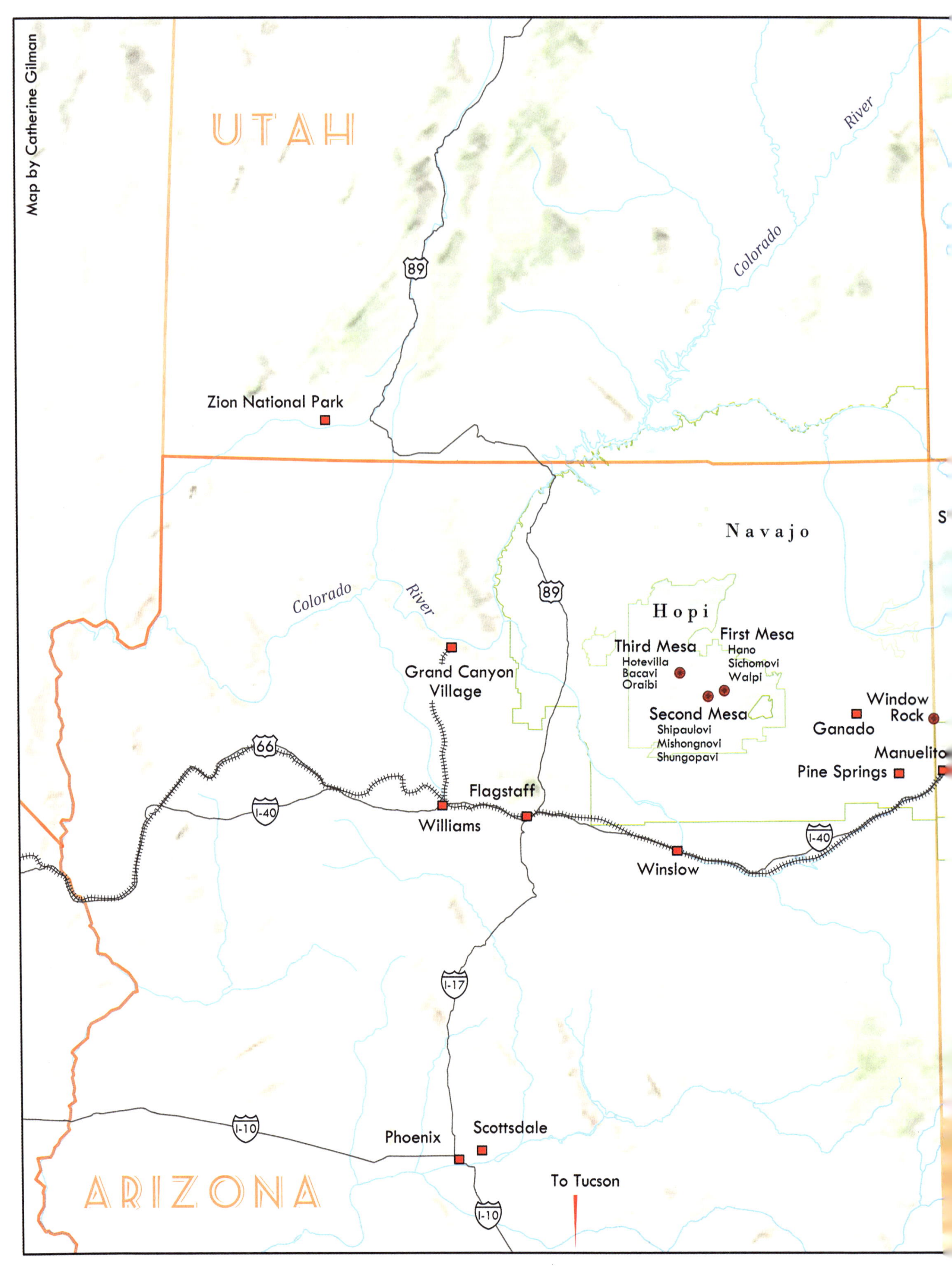

Map by Catherine Gilman
UTAH
Colorado
River
89
Zion National Park
Navajo
Colorado
River
89
Hopi
Third Mesa
Hotevilla
Bacavi
Oraibi
First Mesa
Hano
Sichomovi
Walpi
Second Mesa
Shipaulovi
Mishongnovi
Shungopavi
Grand Canyon
Village
Window
Rock
Ganado
Manuelito
Pine Springs
66
I-40
Flagstaff
Williams
Winslow
I-40
I-17
I-10
Phoenix
Scottsdale
To Tucson
I-10
ARIZONA